Inspirations for a Brighter Day

Volume I

FAY THOMPSON

BIG MOOSE PUBLISHING

ISBN 978-1-7752300-0-7 (paperback)
ISBN 978-17752300-1-4 (electronic book)

Big Moose Publishing 01/2018

For Mom,
with love.

CONTENTS

ACKNOWLEDGEMENTS

This book has been such fun to compile. I thank my friends who repeatedly told me to put these daily inspirations into book form. Bonnie Bogner and Lauren Heistad specifically gave me a message from Spirit nudging me to create this. Little did I know the joy that would bring into my life. Thank you ladies.

I thank all my friends of Facebook who read and continue to read my daily inspirations. You encouraged me to keep going after the first year. Without you, this book would not exist.

A special thanks to Jennifer Sparks who blazed the trail and inspired me to create my own publishing imprint. Big Moose Publishing makes me giggle every time I think of it. I never would have thought I could have done this. Thank you for making it look so easy.

I also wish to thank my wonderful husband, Richard, who is my greatest support. Thank you for always believing in me.

HOW THIS BOOK CAME INTO BEING

Since the fall of 2013, I have been writing a daily inspiration on Facebook. Every morning I sit at my computer and ask for an inspiration. Then, I write whatever comes to me.

Each day is an original gift given to me from the Universe to share with the world.

After a few years of doing this practice, several friends of mine began saying to me that I should make a book out of these daily inspirations. Each of these friends received this message independently from one another. I realized the Universe was desperately trying to get me to hear this message. I have finally decided to listen.

This is the first of several volumes that I plan to publish. It has been a joy to write them. It has been a greater joy to compile them into a volume of work. It is my hope and intent that this book provide you with timely insight and give you just the message you need to hear when you need to hear it. May these inspirations fill your life with joy, harmony, contentment, insight, and new awareness.

If you wish to follow the latest inspirations, please go to www.facebook.com/faythompsoninspires.

HOW TO USE THIS BOOK

This book can be utilized in many ways. Feel free to use it any way that inspires you for your personal use. Some suggestions are as follows:

You can read it from front to back.

You can use it as a daily meditative practice, making notes of what messages and guidance may come to you while you ponder each individual message.

You can use this book like your own personal Magic 8 Ball. Ask a question and open to a page. See what it says.

You can also ask a generic question such as, "What inspiration in this book would be most beneficial for me to pay attention to today?" Then, flip to a page and see what is there.

You can ask what page holds the message that would be most beneficial and contributive to you. Whatever number you receive, turn to that page and read.

You can flip to the Table of Contents, run your finger down

the list until your finger stops. See where you are at, then go to that page.

You can also ask for what letter of the alphabet your message starts with. Go to the table of contents, which is listed alphabetically, to the letter you received, and run your finger down the list until your finger stops. That will be your message.

No matter how you use this book, have fun. Take it lightly and read with an open mind. There is no right or wrong way. Just do what is fun for you.

After reading the inspiration, you may wish to take a moment to apply what you've read. Many of the inspirations contain questions to ponder or actions to carry out. Really allow yourself to apply whatever is being suggested. Change can only happen by changing our usual habits and thought patterns. These inspirations are designed to do that, but will only yield results if you are willing to truly surrender to what is being offered. I urge you to just take a moment to see how the message applies to you and your life.

Finally, when asking yourself the questions given in these inspirations, allow the awareness to come from your heart and your knowing. Your knowing does not come from your head. You do not think when you are acting from knowing. The object is to function from awareness and your knowing – instead of thinking about it. Keep your head out of it. Always go with, "What do I know?"

P.S. – You always know everything you need to know. If you find yourself saying, "I don't know", relax, breathe, and trust that you do know. Ask yourself, "If I did know, which I do, what would it be?" Allow the answer to come from somewhere other than your head. It will if you let it. Your knowing is always present.

P.P.S. – No matter what inspiration you receive, please never use it to judge you or others. They are meant to illuminate what choices you have been making, so that you can get a better understanding of why things are the way they are for you, and open space for you to either be just as you are or change if that is what you desire. They are not meant to judge you or your choices as right or wrong.

ABUNDANCE

The Universe is infinitely abundant and at your service. But, sometimes it doesn't feel that way. It feels more like you got the short end of the stick or were forgotten completely. Here's a secret about how the Universe hands out its abundance: it matches exactly the energy you give it. Feel love in your heart, and the Universe will match that and hand it back with more. Feel rich in your being, and the Universe will match that and hand over riches. Feel beautiful, and the match is more beauty. Feel victimized, unloved, and hurt, and, so too, will these things be matched. It's just a match to your energy, not a slight or a punishment. Knowing this, can you now dip into the infinite abundance the Universe has to offer by giving it what you'd like it to match?

NOTES:

_____

_____

_____

_____

_____

_____

ACKNOWLEDGE THE BLESSING YOU ARE

Who are some of the people in your life that you care about? Are you a blessing to them? Truly allow the truth to reveal itself. If you have doubts, the fact that you care about them is a blessing to them. Many of us are running around trying to pretend we are a wart on the skin of someone's life, when really we are a beauty mark. When we finally acknowledge we are a blessing, we can experience it; and, our world will change. Thank you for the blessing that you are to those you love and to this world.

NOTES:

_____

_____

_____

_____

_____

_____

_____

ADVENTURE

Life is an adventure - what great and fun adventures might you have today? Or, have you decided your life is not an adventure, because you have every minute planned out, and you already know exactly how today is going to go? Would you be willing to allow for some uncertainty in today? Would you allow for it to surprise you with something greater and more fun? Would you be willing to make today, and everyday, an adventure?

NOTES:

_____

_____

_____

_____

_____

_____

_____

_____

_____

ALCHEMY

Alchemy occurs when you leave one vibration for another. Leave worry for faith. Leave doubt for confidence. Leave fear for love. You have the entire Universe making a path for you to follow. You will know the path by the way it feels. The path of alchemy feels delightful, easy, and light-filled. Go towards those feelings, and you will be well on your way. The alchemist is one who laughs and is irreverent. The alchemist is joyful and unattached to outcomes. The alchemist knows s/he will create something wonderful. It is time to put your magic to work. Make a decision to do something daring and inspiring. Be the alchemist today.

NOTES:

_____

_____

_____

_____

_____

_____

_____

ALLOW WHAT IS

Allow for whatever is without judging it as right or wrong. So what if you feel crappy? Allow yourself 5 minutes to feel as crappy as you can. Instead of fighting what is going on with you, as if it is wrong, allow it to be in full force for a specific amount of time. You will likely find you get very bored or annoyed of being that way before your 5 minutes is up. Then, you will change it. Fighting it makes it linger and linger. Allow what is and let it have its moment. Then, move on.

NOTES:

_____

_____

_____

_____

_____

_____

_____

_____

ARE YOU A CREATION MICROMANAGER?

Sometimes we forget what our job is when creating with the Universe. Our job is the what. What do I desire? What is to be my life? But our silly selves decide the infinite Universe is incompetent, or worse - scheming against us — and so we start telling it how to do its job. We start micromanaging the Universe. The Universe's job is to give us how and when. When left to its own devices, the Universe does a much better job than we ever could. If things aren't happening fast enough for you, then, you have decided to take over the timing of your creation. Not your job. Step back and trust. If you are trying to figure out how to make something happen, stop. That's not your job, either. Step back and trust. Do your job. Let the Universe do its job. Focus on what is coming, not on how or when. Do this and life gets easier - magical even.

NOTES:

_____

_____

_____

_____

_____

ARE YOU BEATING YOURSELF WITH THE SAME OLD STICK?

Often we judge ourselves over and over again in the same old ways. "I'm not beautiful." or "I am an outsider." or "No one will want me.".... and the list goes on and on. Today, I challenge you to find one way you beat yourself with the same old stick, and say, "Enough of that. I'm awesome. I don't deserve these insults and I won't have them anymore!" Truly, what if you stopped beating yourself up and looked at how to nurture and empower yourself instead? I wonder what change that may bring? Are you willing to find out?

NOTES:

_____

_____

_____

_____

_____

_____

_____

_____

ARE YOU DISMISSING YOURSELF?

How many of us have been dismissed or ignored as if our input does not matter or contribute, or as if we are irrelevant? What this does is create a pattern of us dismissing ourselves as if we are irrelevant, all the while screaming to be heard. Would you be willing to no longer dismiss yourself? Imagine the time when you were first dismissed and allow yourself to be heard, hugged, and seen in that moment. Then, allow yourself to be heard, hugged, and seen in this moment.

NOTES:

_____

_____

_____

_____

_____

_____

_____

ARE YOU DONE BEING A MARTYR?

A martyr is someone who would give up their life for their beliefs. I wonder if someone is better able to live by their beliefs and create change than to die for them? I mean, when you're dead, people can go on believing whatever they want, just as they can when you are alive, right? Where are you killing yourself for a belief that is not worth it? Where are you being a martyr just so that you can be right and righteous? Is it worth it? Can you believe what you believe without needing to die or care if others won't buy it? Hmmm.....

NOTES:

_____

_____

_____

_____

_____

_____

_____

_____

ARE YOU FOCUSED ON POSSIBILITY OR IMPOSSIBILITY?

Often, when we wish for something, we look at what might cause it not to happen and try to remove that. That's focusing on all the things that make it not possible. What if you solely focused on the possibility of something happening or coming into being? What if it wasn't your job to remove obstacles? What if obstacles are only distractions to the clear path to success? When you focus on possibility, there are no obstacles. They all move out of the way, because when you focus on possibility, there is nothing that can stop you.

NOTES:

_____

_____

_____

_____

_____

_____

_____

_____

ARE YOU JUDGING JUDGMENT?

As we strive to move out of judgment, one common thing we do is make judgment wrong, which, of course, is judgment of judgment. Can you allow for judgment without allowing the judgments to affect you? What we resist persists. Therefore, everywhere we try to get rid of judgment, we are resisting it, which keeps it persistent in our field of energy. Do not worry about the presence of judgments. They will not affect you unless you judge them.

NOTES:

_____

_____

_____

_____

_____

_____

_____

_____

_____

ARE YOU OUTSOURCING?

Since you are the creator of your life, you are the source of your creations. You are in constant connection with God-force, or the Universe, or whatever it is you wish to call it. You are the Source! It is not separate from you. If you think you receive from an outside source, you are denying your own divine power and infinite resources. You are limiting yourself. You are telling yourself you're lacking. When you look to a source outside yourself, you are connecting to a finite source, which will only weaken you, cause you to compromise, or deny you. The true source within you does not ever deny you, judge you, or bargain with you. And, it never is lacking. Stop outsourcing. Go within. You will find everything you need without needing to give up part of you to get it.

NOTES:

_____

_____

_____

_____

_____

_____

ARE YOU TRYING?

Trying is a weird energy that makes it seem like you are making progress toward a goal, but you never get there. Trying constantly keeps you trying. When you finally choose to be something or make something happen, then it happens. Dump trying for choosing. Dump trying for being. Don't try to make things happen. Make things happen.

NOTES:

_____

_____

_____

_____

_____

_____

_____

_____

_____

_____

ARE YOU TRYING TO FULFILL SOMEONE ELSE'S WANTS?

Wherever you have decided you just want other people to be happy, you may unwittingly have attempted to be what they want. Unfortunately, this never really works because you can't make someone else happy. Happiness must come from within. Also, by attempting to be what another wants, you are not being what you desire to be, which will make you unhappy. This, then, makes the world a less happy place. Stop trying to make others happy. You are not the cause nor the solution to someone else's unhappiness. Instead, focus solely on your own happiness, for the sake of the world.

NOTES:

_____

_____

_____

_____

_____

_____

_____

ARE YOU TRYING TO SAVE THE WORLD?

What is the world to you? Is it the earth? Is it a group of people? Is it something else? Does it really need you to save it? How much judgment do you have to have in order to decide you can save the world or the people in it? Are you being a missionary, when people are actually like, "I didn't know I needed saving. I don't want your saving. And, I didn't ask for it, either."? When you stop trying to save the world, you are saved, because you can now put your energy into creating and enjoying your own life, instead of fixing everyone else's.

NOTES:

ARE YOU WILLING TO CHANGE?

Often people say that they want things to change, and are willing to change, but when the time comes for them to choose something different or to do things a different way, they refuse. Change in your life requires you to change. This is an absolute requirement. So, what have you been wishing to change, but refusing to change, because it would require that you change? Would you be willing to change you to gain the change you desire? Or do you wish to keep putting up with the crap you have been creating?

NOTES:

_____

_____

_____

_____

_____

_____

_____

_____

ASSERTIVENESS

Be assertive with your thoughts, your love, and your needs today. Be kind to yourself in a way you never have before. Take a moment to assert how wonderful, kind, and caring a person you are. You have a big heart. Show it off. Stand firm in your conviction of this. Never be afraid of your kindness.

NOTES:

_____

_____

_____

_____

_____

_____

_____

_____

_____

_____

BACK TO BASICS

When in doubt, go back to the basics. Breathe. Spend time in nature. Relax. Be in gratitude. Help someone in need. Be kind. Be kind to you. When you do, the rest will take care of itself. It's simple. Don't make it complicated.

NOTES:

_____

_____

_____

_____

_____

_____

_____

_____

_____

_____

_____

_____

BEAUTY

Stop believing you are not beautiful. You are. What if what you thought was ugly was actually part of your greatest beauty? What if you stopped demanding you aren't beautiful and started demanding that you are? Beauty needs to be acknowledged to be noticed. What if your failure to recognize the beauty in you is the only thing keeping you from being the beauty that you are? You are beautiful. Deal with it. And yes, if you are reading this, this message is for you.

NOTES:

_____

_____

_____

_____

_____

_____

_____

_____

BE HERE NOW

Be here, now, in this moment. Not in the moment that happened a second ago. Not in the moment that will happen a second from now. Be here now. When you do, time will stop, and you will be. You will finally realize that you do exist, and you can then stop trying to prove your existence. You will have total awareness of what is in the moment and total gratitude for it. Try it. Be here now.

NOTES:

_____

_____

_____

_____

_____

_____

_____

_____

BE HONEST WITH YOURSELF

We sometimes tell ourselves lies with our mind, because we are afraid of the truth that is held in our soul. Sometimes we are afraid because we know our truth is not going to please someone else, or is not what is expected of us. Sometimes we are afraid because we know our truth will mean we will have to change. Whatever the reason, the fear will keep you in a place of unhappiness and struggle. When you are honest with yourself about your true feelings, the solution reveals itself. When you cast aside other's wants, demands, and truths, and listen to your own, you find your path and your way. Disengage from your mind and feel your truth. Acknowledge your knowing. This is where your solution lies, and the path to your joy revealed.

NOTES:

_____

_____

_____

_____

_____

_____

BE THE INTENSITY OF YOU

Do you shy away because you are afraid of being too much including too loud, too happy, too enthusiastic, too intense, too aware, or too energetic? How long have you believed in the lie that you are too much? Just how can you be too much of you? You can't. Is it time to consider you are being too little of you, and that the solution to the "problem of you" is actually to be more of you...all of you? You've tried being less. Is it working? Would you be willing to be so much of you that other people can't stand the happiness it brings you? If you will never be you, as intensely you as you are, then what is the point? Did you come here to be less?

NOTES:

_____

_____

_____

_____

_____

_____

_____

_____

BE YOURSELF

Be your quirky, crazy, misfit self. It's the best you. Stay true to what's different about you - that's the real you. Be silly. Be happy. Laugh. Don't try to be like others. Don't mimic. Just be you. The unique, different, wonderful you that you are.

NOTES:

_____

_____

_____

_____

_____

_____

_____

_____

_____

_____

_____

BLOSSOMING

Things are getting started for you. Just as a flower needs time to bud, develop and grow, so do you and your projects. Do not let impatience thwart your efforts or make you feel like things aren't happening fast enough. Trust in the process of divine timing. Trust that everything is working out in perfect order and in perfect time. Nurture it and yourself through the process. Don't rush and don't give up. When you do this you will see the flowers blooming faster than you thought possible.

NOTES:

_____

_____

_____

_____

_____

_____

_____

_____

BODY MOVEMENT

If life is stagnant or not moving, then it is time for you to move - literally. When you move your body by stretching, walking, or some other activity, it releases stuck energy, releases toxins, and clears the mind. The message today is to move your body and get that energy flowing. You will feel better. More ideas and solutions will then come your way. Low energy is a sign that your body needs to move. When you go for a walk, dance, or run, you will dramatically increase the amount of energy you have. When energy flows it nourishes, replenishes, and vitalizes you. Today, find some time to move and get those juices flowing!

NOTES:

_____

_____

_____

_____

_____

_____

_____

_____

CATCH 22

A catch 22 is where you are damned if you do and damned if you don't. What if you are not damned at all? What if you call its bluff? When you are no longer controlled by a catch 22, it has no control over you. You are then free to choose. What else is possible other than the two options you have given yourself? Surrender to the possibility that there are more possibilities, and, no matter what, you will not be controlled by this crazy situation any longer. You can break the hold of a catch 22, but you must be willing to go past it.

NOTES:

_____

_____

_____

_____

_____

_____

_____

_____

CHAOS AND ORDER

Chaos is the building block of creation. All creation is made from chaos. Order puts all your ducks in a row and creates the box or the comfort zone that doesn't allow for you to stray from it. It locks you in and limits you. Ask, "How much chaos is required to create the life I love and am excited to wake up to?" Then, invite that chaos in. Continue with, "How much chaos is required to break up the ordered, boring, limited life I am living?" Then, invite that in. Chaos is the stuff that miracles are made of. Invite it in.

NOTES:

_____

_____

_____

_____

_____

_____

_____

_____

CHOICE OVER OBLIGATION

We often fool ourselves into believing obligations are no-choice situations. The truth is, we have chosen the obligations. You don't have to go to your parents for Christmas. You don't have to pretend you like Aunt Gertrude's cooking. You don't have to do anything. You choose to. You have a choice to do something entirely different. You can choose to stay home. You can choose to lie. You can choose to bring a delicious dish to add to Aunt Gertrude's table. There are lots of choices. None of them are wrong. Remember, if you choose to go do something you would rather not, then you could also choose to enjoy it. Just acknowledging that you are making a choice, instead of being forced into a situation, will make you feel exponentially better.

NOTES:

_____

_____

_____

_____

_____

CHOOSING TO CHANGE DOESN'T REQUIRE KNOWING HOW TO CHANGE

When you choose something, the Universe begins working to bring it into existence. You don't need to know how that will happen; you just need to begin by making a demand that "this is changing now!" It may seem scary or worrisome going ahead without knowledge of how it will turn out, but that will be short-lived if you stay on course with conviction. You will be shown the way. Just keep strong in your choice to change, and how will be revealed to you step by step.

NOTES:

_____

_____

_____

_____

_____

_____

_____

_____

COMMITMENT TO KINDNESS

How committed are you to being kind to yourself? How committed are you to being hard on yourself? If the second question holds a greater punch, is it time to switch loyalties? What would it take to be kind to you? What would you have to stop doing, and what lies would you have to stop believing? You are as worthy of kindness as you are worthy of breathing air. Don't short-change yourself on either.

NOTES:

_____

_____

_____

_____

_____

_____

_____

_____

COMMITMENT TO LAUGHTER

What if you committed to laughing everyday, several times a day? No matter the circumstances, no matter the place or time, what if you chose laughter over your usual mood, thoughts, feelings, or emotions? What might change in your life? Might you be forced to let go of complaint or worry? Would you be willing to commit to having laughter in your day, several times a day?

NOTES:

_____

_____

_____

_____

_____

_____

_____

_____

_____

_____

COMMUNICATING FREELY

What do you keep silent in order to keep the peace or avoid judgment? What do you hide in fear that others will ridicule? What dreams are you ignoring because others won't understand how important they are to you? Communicate freely today - at least to yourself - what is important to you. When you get it out in the open it can no longer be ignored. Sometimes life works much better when we stop trying to keep it neat and tidy for other's sake.

NOTES:

_____

_____

_____

_____

_____

_____

_____

_____

COMPLAINING CREATES MORE TO COMPLAIN ABOUT

Complaining never brings change or a solution. It brings more for you to be unhappy about. It stops you from creating something else, because you put your focus on what you are complaining about. It is a time waster, a joy-stealer, and a constant annoyance. Why feed it? Next time you are aware that you are complaining, stop and ask, "What do I really desire here?" Choose to put energy towards having that. Otherwise, you'll be stuck with the crap, and you will always have something to complain about.

NOTES:

_____

_____

_____

_____

_____

_____

_____

COURAGE

Courage is demanding what is right and true for you and choosing it without apology. Courage requires choosing outside the norm, not in defiance, but with humble vulnerability and without needing justification for your choice. So whatever it is, go for it! Do it! No regrets. Stand tall. Have courage.

NOTES:

_____

_____

_____

_____

_____

_____

_____

_____

_____

_____

CREATE

What are you not creating, that you would like to create, that you don't think you should bother creating, because no one would probably like it anyway? How about you? Might you like it? Then, create it. We must stop trying to determine what people will and will not like as a condition of creation. What if it doesn't matter? What if you could just enjoy yourself in the process? What if creating what you like would make you happy?

NOTES:

_____

_____

_____

_____

_____

_____

_____

_____

_____

_____

CURIOSITY

When things seem stagnant or like they are going in the wrong direction, it is time to get curious about other possibilities. Curiosity is the same as asking questions with wonder and sincerity. "I wonder what the best possible course of action is?" "I wonder what the possibilities of this coming to be is?" "I wonder what wonderful things may happen?" "I wonder what I don't know that the Universe can deliver, if I just believe?" When we ask questions with wonder and sincerity, we open up to possibility. New doorways and pathways that were not previously available appear. Be careful not to answer the questions you are asking. Just ask with wonder, and allow the Universe to show you the way. Let the Universe lead you, because, let's face it, if you knew the answer, you wouldn't have to ask the question.

NOTES:

_____

_____

_____

_____

_____

_____

DEFENDING

Everywhere you are defending your rights, your point of view, your possessions, your loved ones, and yourself against that which is unwanted, you create a war with whatever you are trying to win against. The important part here is "you create a war", which means you can also create peace by no longer defending against, judging, making yourself or others wrong, or pretending that others have more power than you. When we let down our defenses, we create receiving, possibility, and miracles. Go ahead. Try it. You might find that there never was a war in the first place.

NOTES:

_____

_____

_____

_____

_____

_____

_____

DEMAND MORE

You never get what you deserve. Instead, you get what you are willing to demand to have. This is not greed. You cannot get greedy with an infinite Universe. You choosing to have more kindness, abundance, money, joy, fun, and laughter in your life does not deplete the Universe of its resources. You having more does not mean there is less to give to others. The Universe is infinite. Demand more in your life. Choose with wild abandon knowing you are creating more in the world and not taking from it.

NOTES:

_____

_____

_____

_____

_____

_____

_____

_____

DETACH FROM THE SITUATION

If you are too attached to a situation or outcome, you will create fear and drama that things may not happen the way you hope. You must release yourself from all worry and expectation, and instead put yourself in a state of faith that all is working out perfectly, and what is to be will be. When you bring this peace within you, your outer situation will change to match that vibration or feeling. Trust in the Universe to work its magic. Trust in yourself to let go. Let go. Let go. Let go. Detach. Detach. Detach. Laugh. Laugh. Laugh. All is well. All is well. All is well.

NOTES:

_____

_____

_____

_____

_____

_____

_____

DISTRACTIONS

How many distractions do you create (and give your energy to) that keep you believing you can't do what you'd really like to do? What if you cut them off and gave them no more time and energy, at least until you give ample energy to creating your desire? What if you put you first for a change? Until you do, you will never find the time for you or your dreams.

NOTES:

_____

_____

_____

_____

_____

_____

_____

_____

_____

DOES YOUR FAITH INCLUDE YOU?

We have all been told to have faith, but in what? If the answer is, "in others", then perhaps we need to check if our faith includes us. The only one you need to have faith in is you - the infinite, magical you. Do you believe in you? Do you have faith in yourself? If your faith doesn't include you, then you will always be trying to prove yourself, including proving your right to exist. God dwells within you and is not separate from you. Faith resides within you. Stop looking for it in other people. It's not there.

NOTES:

_____

_____

_____

_____

_____

_____

_____

_____

DO IT ANYWAY

We hear it all the time. "How can I enjoy myself when I'm worried about _____?" Do it anyway. "How can I be happy when others are not?" Do it anyway. "How can I do what I love when others will judge me?" Do it anyway. There will always be an excuse or a reason for you not to be happy or to not experience something you desire. Do it anyway. If we let our reasons determine our choices, instead of what is in our hearts, we are stuck. To get unstuck, do it anyway.

NOTES:

_____

_____

_____

_____

_____

_____

_____

_____

_____

DO NOT BE CAREFUL WHAT YOU WISH FOR

The saying, "Be careful what you wish for" immediately puts us on guard as though what we wish may be bad. Instead, WISH WITH CAREFREE ABANDON! Wish without worry. Go forth and allow yourself to engage in magical thoughts and possibilities. You just might get it. Release yourself from being careful and walk boldly into the face of creation knowing anything is possible.

NOTES:

_____

_____

_____

_____

_____

_____

_____

_____

DON'T SWEAT THE SMALL STUFF

It's all small stuff. All of it. Anything you make big and important is inflated beyond measure. Even a mountain on an infinite, universal scale is miniscule. So relax. Breathe. And remind yourself that everything is working in your favor. The Universe has your back.

NOTES:

_____

_____

_____

_____

_____

_____

_____

_____

_____

_____

DON'T YOU CARE?

Often when people are upset they want you to make their upset very significant. If you don't, then it is deemed that you don't care. You care. You care so much that you would take on upset in hopes that it would help. It never does. It just makes you feel like crap. Focusing on upset only creates more upset. Care more about a person's happiness than their upset. If they care more about their upset than their happiness, then allow them their choice without making any of it significant.

NOTES:

_____

_____

_____

_____

_____

_____

_____

_____

_____

DO THE OPPOSITE

If you have been trying and trying to make something happen or get something done with no effect and only struggle, perhaps it is time to do the exact opposite of what you have been doing. If you've been being nice and it isn't working, maybe it is time to get mad. If you've been trying to push something away and it won't go, invite it in. Whatever it is, try the exact opposite energy to what you are doing. You may just find you get the exact opposite result of what you are getting now.

NOTES:

_____

_____

_____

_____

_____

_____

_____

_____

DO YOU FEEL TORTURED?

Whatever we put focus upon creates our life. If you feel like a tortured soul, then perhaps you have been focusing more on the unkindness and cruelty in the world, instead of the kindness, gratitude, and blessings. Would you be wiling to give up your fight against unkindness and cruelty, and solely focus on its opposite? The opposite of torture is nurture. What would happen if you focused only on nurturing you and those around you?

NOTES:

_____

_____

_____

_____

_____

_____

_____

_____

DO YOU LIFT YOURSELF UP OR PUSH YOURSELF DOWN?

There seems to be a crazy notion in this world that if you push yourself down and create pressure on top of you, then, somehow, you will find the motivation to fight back and conquer the world. Does that really happen or are you just fighting a war that ultimately leaves you feeling deflated and squashed? What if we applied pressure underneath us and lifted ourselves up, allowing that pressure to make us soar? You never get anywhere good putting yourself down. Never. Try lifting yourself up.

NOTES:

_____

_____

_____

_____

_____

_____

_____

_____

DO YOU UNDERESTIMATE YOURSELF? DO OTHERS UNDERESTIMATE YOU?

What do you love about being underestimated that keeps you choosing it? Is it time to come out of hiding and show the world your brilliance? What if you no longer chose to be underestimated? What joy might be created in your life when the awesomeness of you is recognized and acknowledged? I wonder?

NOTES:

_____

_____

_____

_____

_____

_____

_____

_____

_____

_____

DREAM BIG

You keep yourself small by thinking small. There is nothing in this Universe you can't have. If you can dream it coming into being, you can have it. Do not accept the notion that you have to settle or compromise in order to have a tiny slice of what you want. The Universe is willing to give you the whole pie if you are willing to eat it. The question here is "What are you willing to have?" not "What is available?" The moment you decide what you are willing to have, and believe the Universe will conspire to bring it to you, it is in the works to happen. The moment you decide it is not possible for you, it is in the works to not happen. Your thoughts are that powerful. So, dream big today, own your dreams, and know you can have and will have whatever you are willing to have.

NOTES:

_____

_____

_____

_____

_____

_____

EAT, DRINK, AND BE MERRY

On your deathbed, are you going to regret eating that delicious cake or drinking that marvelous glass of champagne? Are you going to wish you were 10 pounds lighter? Or are you going to smile at all the fun and laughter and enjoyment you had out of life? And, if you don't think there will be much fun, laughter, and enjoyment to look back and smile upon, then might it be an idea to start creating some of that? Eat, drink, and be merry folks. Enjoy life and stop trying to do it right. Just do it fun and all will be well.

NOTES:

_____

_____

_____

_____

_____

_____

_____

_____

ENTHUSIASM

How much enthusiasm do you have for your life? How much enthusiasm would you have if you chose things you loved? When you are enthusiastic anything is possible. You feel energized and as though you can take on the world! Nothing stands in your way. Ask the Universe for enthusiasm and for things that will make you enthusiastic. If you don't ask, you don't receive. Then, get the energy of what that will be like. Enthusiasm will be on its way.

NOTES:

_____

_____

_____

_____

_____

_____

_____

_____

_____

EXPECTING MIRACLES

Miracles happen – all the time – everyday. Feel the anticipation of something good coming your way. Where are you closing doors to joy? Open them. Where are you harboring resentment? Let it wash away at sea. Miracles come when you are open to them. Expect them. It is the same as when you invite a friend over and you expect them to show up. You feel joyful that they are coming to visit. You are happy and prepare for their arrival. Expect your friend the miracle. Feel the joy of it coming to visit. Prepare for its arrival!

NOTES:

_____

_____

_____

_____

_____

_____

_____

EXPLORE THE FORBIDDEN

What energies have you forbade you to experience, or explore? What energies have you never allowed for yourself, or resist? Close your eyes and find the energy that you just never go to, but wish you could. Pull at it. Explore it. What if you allowed for it? What is it? Is it exactly what you've been looking for? Is it exactly what needs attention and to be dealt with? You may be surprised how important and necessary those forbidden energies are to your well-being.

NOTES:

_____

_____

_____

_____

_____

_____

_____

_____

_____

FACE FEAR IN THE FACE

The funny thing about fear is that it makes us cower and not want to face it, but as soon as we do, we realize that it actually is afraid of us. The moment we stand up to it, it moves out of our way quickly. What if you just stood up to the very thing you fear most? What if you chose to no longer fear it? Then, you might have to stop using it as an excuse as to why you can't do the things you wish you could, or have the things you wish you had.

NOTES:

_____

_____

_____

_____

_____

_____

_____

_____

FEELINGS VERSUS BEING

Feelings are a lower version of being. When you focus on being, you become. When you focus on feelings, you feel. Becoming is far more powerful than feeling. For instance, feel happy. Get the energy of feeling happy. Now, be happy. Is it different? Completely. What can you be today that you were only hoping to feel? Go for gold. Be.

NOTES:

_____

_____

_____

_____

_____

_____

_____

_____

_____

_____

FIGHTING JOY

How much energy do you use to fight off the ease and joy that the universe is constantly offering you? How much do we demand that life IS hard and the harder the better, damn it!? Seems ridiculous when we put it into words, yet the truth of it comes through. What if joy isn't the enemy? What if there is no enemy? What if you just chose to enjoy yourself today, instead of fighting your way to it?

NOTES:

_____

_____

_____

_____

_____

_____

_____

_____

_____

FINISH

Finishing gives one a sense of accomplishment, completion, and pride in one's work. Finishing gives you a finished product. Without the finish, you have nothing to show for your efforts and creativity. What would it take to finish what you started? What might you have to acknowledge if you actually finished the project that you started with gusto, and then, just left hanging? Would you be willing to allow you to experience the value and joy of the finish?

NOTES:

_____

_____

_____

_____

_____

_____

_____

_____

FIRSTS

When we are young, we go through many firsts - first steps, first grade, first kiss, etc. Life is an adventure when we have firsts in it. Firsts bring new experiences and insights. The challenge, as we grow older, is to continue having firsts. When we do, we feel alive and young again. What firsts can you bring into your life today and into your tomorrows? You are never too old for a first.

NOTES:

_____

_____

_____

_____

_____

_____

_____

_____

FOLLOW THE LIGHT INSTEAD OF FIXING THE DARK

How often do we search for problems to fix or solve? How often do we take what is heavy and dark, and try to change it to light, instead of realizing it is a heavy, dark road and time to change course? If we would take the dark at face value and go into a different, lighter direction, we would create a lot more ease and a lot less trouble in our lives. Next time you are stuck trying to fix something, stop. What if you didn't need to fix it? What if it is just letting you know to change course?

NOTES:

_____

_____

_____

_____

_____

_____

_____

FORGIVENESS

Truc forgiveness is releasing all judgment about an event or occurrence. To truly be free of it, you must let go of how right you are that it shouldn't have happened and how wrong it was for it to have happened. It happened. Judgment keeps you locked in a death loop that tries to change the event that cannot be changed. Forgiveness allows you to move on. What would it take for you to forgive all your past hurts, pains, and blames especially the ones you hold yourself accountable for? What freedom might that give you?

NOTES:

_____

_____

_____

_____

_____

_____

_____

_____

FREEDOM

Exercise your freedom to choose today. If you have decided you don't have a choice, it is only because you chose it that way. What if you do have not only a choice, but infinite choices? What if you broke away from the conformity and chose something different that made you feel free? A life spent trying to fit in is a life spent limiting yourself and putting yourself in a box. Break out of the box today and experience the freedom of choosing something different. Experience the freedom of exercising choice.

NOTES:

_____

_____

_____

_____

_____

_____

_____

_____

FRIENDSHIP

Did you know you can recognize a true friend by these 3 things?

1. They allow you to be you and never ask you to be someone you are not.

2. They always have your back no matter what, and

3. They never judge you.

How good of a friend are you to you? Are you your own best friend? If you're not, how do you expect someone else to be? What could you do or be different today to be a better friend to you?

NOTES:

_____

_____

_____

_____

_____

_____

_____

GENEROSITY

When you are feeling generous, you feel as though you have more than enough. You feel you will not lose in the act of giving, and that you have something of value to give. These are GREAT energies to be telling the Universe, because the Universe will have to match them and bring them back to you - always making sure you have more than enough, that you gain in the act of giving, and that you are valuable. Be generous today. Be generous in your kindness and compliments to yourself as well, and watch your abundance grow and grow!

NOTES:

_____

_____

_____

_____

_____

_____

_____

GENEROSITY OF SPIRIT

Where do you hold back? What do you have to give that you have decided is not enough, so you don't? Where do you deny the world of the wonder of you? Generosity of spirit has to do with giving of self - not in a way that you are depleted after the giving, but in a way that creates more for all involved. When you truly give generously of you, you are expanded. You are infinite and there is no end to what you are and what you have to give. Don't deny the world of your wonder in fear that you won't have enough left over for you, or because you think that what you have to give is lacking. What can you give today that would allow you to receive the message of how infinitely magnificent and generous you are?

NOTES:

_____

_____

_____

_____

_____

_____

GET HONEST WITH YOURSELF

Where are you harboring judgments or resentments? What is nagging at you that you keep ignoring? What are you pretending isn't there that is? When we get honest with ourselves we have a chance to resolve old hurts and grievances and finally let them go forever. Hiding them does not make them disappear. Be honest and let yourself let go and have peace.

NOTES:

_____

_____

_____

_____

_____

_____

_____

_____

GETTING YOUNG

What if we stopped telling and believing the story that we are getting older? What would happen if we focused upon getting younger? Just try that on for a moment. Does your world feel lighter and more energized? I wonder what magic we might be able to create and experience if we asked the Universe to prepare us for youth?

NOTES:

_____

_____

_____

_____

_____

_____

_____

_____

_____

_____

GIFT OF LIFE

What if life was an incredible gift you are not unwrapping? How many of us refuse to unwrap it? How long do you have to wait to open it? When is that time? When you get a degree? When you get married? When you retire? When you're dead? How about now? What would happen if you opened it now? Don't make your life a do-not-open gift. Open and enjoy this gift now.

NOTES:

_____

_____

_____

_____

_____

_____

_____

_____

_____

GO FOR AWARENESS INSTEAD OF ADVICE

When you ask for other people's advice, you are getting their point of view. They put themselves in your situation, and tell you what they would do. While most often well intentioned, advice rarely takes into account what is the most beneficial to you. What if, instead of asking for advice, you asked for awareness? Asking for awareness is asking to see the whole situation clearly as it pertains to everyone involved. Awareness will show what is beneficial to you and what is not. Take a moment to ask the Universe to give you awareness everywhere you have been seeking advice. What do you become aware of?

NOTES:

_____

_____

_____

_____

_____

_____

GO FOR IT

Sometimes to make things happen you need to make things happen. Go for it! Leap! Take the risk! Just do it without thinking. Thinking talks you out of the fun. Thinking talks you out of the possibilities. Go and trust the excitement making such a decision gives you. It's letting you know that it will work out. So, GO FOR IT!

NOTES:

_____

_____

_____

_____

_____

_____

_____

_____

_____

_____

GOING BEYOND

You are an infinite being who can go beyond anything. Nothing is out of your reach. Anything is possible. What dreams are you not dreaming because they are beyond your imagination? What choices are you not making because they are beyond your capability? These are lies. Play with going beyond today. Exercise the muscle of going beyond. You may find you go much further than you ever thought possible.

NOTES:

_____

_____

_____

_____

_____

_____

_____

_____

_____

_____

GO OUTSIDE

It is time to go outside, breathe in the fresh air, and air out your mind and body. Nothing is more cleansing and refreshing than being outdoors in nature. Even if it is for a short time, go outdoors with the intent of being refreshed and renewed. Go for a walk, feel the breeze on your skin, listen to the birds chirping, and enjoy! If you feel unmotivated to get outside, force yourself to go. That's when you need it the most. Fresh air will bring fresh ideas and fresh feelings. Enjoy.

NOTES:

_____

_____

_____

_____

_____

_____

_____

_____

GRATEFUL FOR YOU

When we think of what we are grateful for, we often forget about ourselves. Would you be willing to take a moment to be grateful for who you truly are? Would you be willing to be grateful for the laughter and kindness you bring to this world? Would you be willing to be grateful for you - just as you are - no matter what you are or are not choosing? This is self-love. Let's have a little of that...or a lot...

NOTES:

_____

_____

_____

_____

_____

_____

_____

_____

GREATER OR GREATER THAN

There is a difference to wishing to be greater and wishing to be greater than. Being greater means you come into more of your true self - the infinite greatness that you truly are. Wishing to be greater than puts you in comparison with others and always diminishes you or someone else. You cannot be compared to anything or anything to you. You are incomparable. When you truly receive that truth, you will be greater.

NOTES:

_____

_____

_____

_____

_____

_____

_____

_____

_____

HAPPINESS FOR NO REASON

If you choose happiness for no reason at all then it can never be taken away from you for any reason. You become invincible. Choosing happiness for happiness' sake, and not because you did the right thing, or because you got lucky, or because someone else did what you wanted, allows you to no longer be slave to life needing to be a certain way. You no longer have to chase happiness. Choose happiness for happiness' sake. Choose happiness for no reason at all, and let no reason come between you and that choice.

NOTES:

_____

_____

_____

_____

_____

_____

_____

_____

HAPPY SURPRISE

Today, like any other day, is full of happy surprises. Happy surprises come when we have no expectations about what we think will or should happen. They happen when we greet the day with gratitude, wonder, and curiosity. Today, instead of deciding how the day is going to be, release all expectation. Imagine how wonderful the day could be if you went into it wide-eyed, full of wonder and joy, and expecting nothing. See this day as a child does, like an adventure!

NOTES:

_____

_____

_____

_____

_____

_____

_____

_____

HAVE WHAT YOU DON'T DESERVE

How many of us deny ourselves on the premise that we don't deserve it? How many of us deny others of kindness or forgiveness because they don't deserve it? What if deserving really has nothing to do with it? What if being bold enough to say, "I'm having kindness and generosity and mercy and grace and abundance and all the other things I 'don't' deserve" is the way to creating those things in our lives and in the world? We must forget about deserving and start being. We all deserve kindness. We all deserve happiness. The only reason we might not have it is because we haven't chose it, or we believed some stupid idea that we don't deserve it.

NOTES:

_____

_____

_____

_____

_____

_____

_____

HAVE YOU TOLD YOURSELF HOW AWESOME YOU ARE LATELY?

You are awesome. How often in a day do you forget? How often in a day do you insult, belittle, or curse yourself? You're too awesome for that. Even the most awesome people do silly or stupid stuff - but then laugh. It's just part of being awesome. Today, will you finally stop lying to yourself with your criticisms and insults and start telling the truth, proclaiming at the top of your lungs, "DAMN, I'M AWESOME!"?

NOTES:

_____

_____

_____

_____

_____

_____

_____

_____

_____

HELLO AND GOODBYE

Change requires these two greetings. Hello to something new. Goodbye to the old way. Remember, if you are stuck saying good-bye, then, it is difficult to properly greet your newfound change with a hello. So, what have you been saying goodbye to for far too long? What have you left waiting to be greeted with open arms? Is it time for hello?

NOTES:

_____

_____

_____

_____

_____

_____

_____

_____

_____

_____

HOW EASY ARE YOU WILLING TO LET YOUR LIFE GET?

Are you willing to allow your life to be easy? Would you be willing to let go of the lie that life would be boring if it were easy? Think of all the times when things were easy for you. Were you ever bored? I'm guessing not. I'm guessing you were happy, creative, energized, and playful. So, how easy are you willing to allow your life to get?

NOTES:

_____

_____

_____

_____

_____

_____

_____

_____

HOW HARD ARE YOU ON YOURSELF?

Somewhere along the line the lie was told that if you are hard on yourself, you will become a better person. Is that true? Or is it that you make yourself a more punished and tortured person? Are you done abusing yourself in the name of bettering yourself or proving yourself? Wouldn't you be better if you treated yourself kindly? Is it time that you gave up being hard on yourself, and, instead, truly honored and supported yourself with kindness?

NOTES:

_____

_____

_____

_____

_____

_____

_____

_____

HOW MUCH FUN CAN I HAVE TODAY?

Do you ever ask yourself this question - I mean, really ask it? Or do you go to the foregone conclusion that fun isn't happening in your day, because today is like any other day? What if it isn't? What if it could be something else, if you allowed for it? How much would you need to lighten up and relax in order for fun to happen? How much attitude around being right about how boring or troubled your life is, would you have to let go of in order to allow fun in your life? I wonder if you can really ask this today in a way that the possibility of it must show up – "How much fun can I have today? I wonder?"

NOTES:

_____

_____

_____

_____

_____

_____

_____

HOW MUCH IS HOW MUCH YOU LIKE YOU BASED ON ANOTHER'S OPINION?

This is a great question to ponder. For many the answer is close to the 100% mark. Are you ready to change that? Are you willing to no longer base what you like on other's opinions? Are you willing to be that bold and daring? To like yourself without regard for another's opinion is a renegade move in this reality. It is viewed as dangerous, because if you truly like yourself despite other's opinions, then no one has control over you, your joy, your pleasure, or your happiness. Are you willing to be that different? Are you willing to be that uncontrollable? Hint: You already are that different. Is it time to like yourself for that fact?

NOTES:

_____

_____

_____

_____

_____

_____

_____

HOW OFTEN DO YOU SMILE?

Ever pay attention to this? Ever realize that maybe you smile a lot less than you might like to? What if you just decided to smile more? What if you just threw caution to the wind, lowered your barriers, lightened up, and smiled right in the face of all your problems, woes, upsets, and worries? What if when you choose to smile (and I mean really smile, not a forced grin through gritted teeth), you create a different energy and a different reality? You might just create a life worth smiling about.

NOTES:

_____

_____

_____

_____

_____

_____

_____

_____

I DID IT MY WAY

How often do you make your way the wrong way or go the other extreme with my way or the highway? Your way is the most precious gift you can give yourself, and it is only for you. Others won't take to your way because they have their way, which is a precious gift to them. All of us are running around, trying to find someone doing it their way so that we can copy it, and have the same success as them. It doesn't work. Today, if you knew of no other way, what would you do? What is your way? If your way doesn't work, then try a different way. You may find it didn't work, because you copied it from someone else. Be unique. Be different. Be you. Do it your way.

NOTES:

_____

_____

_____

_____

_____

_____

IF YOU ARE FIGHTING FOR SOMETHING, YOU'VE ALREADY LOST

We have been taught to fight for everything we want. Fighting requires struggle, hardship, pain, enemies, and often loss. What if you didn't need to fight? What if you could just choose? What if you could trust the Universe to open the way for you and show you every step? Would you be willing to stop fighting and start choosing?

NOTES:

_____

_____

_____

_____

_____

_____

_____

_____

_____

IF YOU WERE MARRIED TO YOU, WOULD YOU WANT A DIVORCE?

All of our relationships stem from the relationship we have with our own self. If we do not treat ourselves kindly, we will not be able to receive kindness from others. If we do not treat ourselves with gratitude, we will not be able to receive the gratitude of others. Is it time to work on your relationship with yourself, which is the core of all your relationships? If you were married to you, would you want a divorce? If so, what could you do to let you know that you are adored? What would it take for you to feel like the luckiest person in the world to have you in your corner, cheering you on?

NOTES:

_____

_____

_____

_____

_____

_____

I HAVE TO

The phrase "I have to" always leaves you feeling obligated, and never allows you to choose for yourself. You don't have to do anything. You choose everything. What are you choosing as the "I have to's" of your life that really are the "I could choose this or not's" of your life? Would you allow yourself options?

NOTES:

_____

_____

_____

_____

_____

_____

_____

_____

_____

_____

I'M NOT HAPPY ABOUT THAT

Whenever you hear yourself saying or thinking "I'm not happy about that," then it is time to ask, "What would it take for me to be happy right now?" We have all sorts of excuses as to why we cannot be happy. Are they relevant? Is the fact that the toast burned worth your happiness? Is the fact that the guy you work with likes to be a jerk worth your happiness? How can you find the humor and ridiculousness of and in it all? How might you be able to be happy in the midst of things that you have decided you are not happy about?

NOTES:

_____

_____

_____

_____

_____

_____

_____

_____

IN FRONT OF YOUR FACE

Sometimes when you think you are lacking, or when you don't have a clue what to do next, it is because what you need is right in front of your face. You aren't getting clues, because what you need is sitting right there. You think you are lacking because you aren't acknowledging what you have. Instead of seeking, start taking inventory. What do you have? It might be a friend or support you take for granted. It might be skills and abilities you discount, because they seem too easy. It might be the simple task of getting quiet and just allowing yourself to be. What if you aren't lacking? What if what you need is right in front of your face?

NOTES:

_____

_____

_____

_____

_____

_____

_____

_____

INNER POWER

Draw on your own inner power today. You have more strength than you can imagine, I promise. Whatever it is that is troubling you, access your gratitude, strength, and potency from within. Stop trying to figure it out, because, power does not come out of your head. Your mind doesn't hold your strength. You do, and you access it from your very core. Have faith in yourself, and trust that you can find a better way. A better way will be, when you demand it to be. That is the power of your potency.

NOTES:

_____

_____

_____

_____

_____

_____

_____

_____

IRREVERENT

If there is one piece of advice I can give as a life coach, it is to be irreverent. The definition of irreverent is "showing a lack of respect for people or things that are generally taken seriously". We take far too much seriously. We don't laugh or have fun near enough. We make people and things very significant. This doesn't allow for us to be silly, light-hearted, or carefree. It is actually disrespectful to steal our joy by asking us to take things seriously. Be irreverent and relax. Make nothing so serious that you can't have fun or be joyful.

NOTES:

_____

_____

_____

_____

_____

_____

_____

_____

IS IT TIME?

Timing plays into the creation of a miracle. We often are impatient, and want to push to have what we want right now. Sometimes, a greater result will occur by being patient and waiting for the perfect time. When things don't seem to be going as fast as you wish, you may want to ask, "Is now the time?" You may need to leave room for it to breathe and become more. You can't force a flower to open before it is ready. Don't try to force your miracles, your creations, and your magic. It all comes easily in perfect time. Let it.

NOTES:

_____

_____

_____

_____

_____

_____

_____

_____

_____

IS IT TIME TO STOP ACTING?

You play many roles in your life. What if you stopped playing roles, and were present as yourself in each moment? Would that be a greater gift to the world, even if it may be an adjustment? Perhaps it is time to stop pretending we know it all, or have it all together, or are happy to serve other people's every whim, or are a Stepford wife, or a impenetrable fortress, or.... Are you getting the idea? What if you just were honest with yourself and present with others as yourself? No roles. No acting. No playing your part. Just being real. I wonder what that might be like....

NOTES:

_____

_____

_____

_____

_____

_____

_____

_____

IS IT TIME TO UP THE ANTE?

What's your usual level of joy? Is it near enough? Is it time to up the ante and allow for you to be more joyful? Joy is a choice. Happiness is a choice. Joy doesn't come from an outside source. For it to increase, you have to let go of your regular way of being and choose to be more joyful for no reason at all. We must never look for someone or something else to sustain it, or increase it. Go ahead. Up the ante. Is it a risk? Yes, but one that pays off.

NOTES:

_____

_____

_____

_____

_____

_____

_____

_____

_____

IS THIS ABOUT YOU?

Often when people are mean or nasty to us, we decide it must be because we did something wrong. We don't consider that, perhaps, it has nothing to do with us. A great question to ask when you feel this way is, "Is this about me?" Usually, it isn't. Others will tell you it is because they are refusing to look within themselves. It is not your job to fix other's upsets. Don't make yourself the cause of them, because you are not. It's not about you. Instead, move on and wish them blessings knowing we all get grumpy from time to time.

NOTES:

_____

_____

_____

_____

_____

_____

_____

_____

IS THIS RELEVANT?

We often become distracted by problems or issues that are not relevant to what we wish to create. Whenever you feel pulled away from happiness, joy, ease or creation, ask, "Is this relevant?" Most often it is not. If it's not, do not give it your time and energy. Go back to creating and working in the world of possibilities. What's relevant is your desire. Keep your eye on the prize.

NOTES:

_____

_____

_____

_____

_____

_____

_____

_____

_____

_____

IS THIS THE CHANGE YOU HAVE BEEN ASKING FOR?

Sometimes when things feel awful or are seemingly going wrong, you might want to ask, "Is this the change I have been asking for?" Sometimes things seemingly get "worse" so that you can spot what needs to be let go of. Comfort does not create the environment for change. If you were always comfortable with what you have, why change it? It sometimes has to become a nuisance so that you will finally look at it and release it. Remember, "worse" is not always worse. It sometimes is exactly what is needed. The sooner you let it go, the sooner it leaves.

NOTES:

_____

_____

_____

_____

_____

_____

IT'S JOY TIME!

How long have you had your nose to the grindstone? Is it time to take a break and have some joy time? How often in a day do you think about having joy time? Is the number a little low? What if you made a commitment to increasing it? Your life is right now. It is not in the future, and not in the glory days of the past. It's right now. If you would like joy, then create it right now. And please know you do not need to suffer and toil away in order to create it. Suffering and toiling create hardship and effort, and joy does not spring from it. Joy springs from the absence of it. Give yourself a gift today. Proclaim that it is JOY TIME!

NOTES:

_____

_____

_____

_____

_____

_____

_____

IT'S NOT A PROBLEM TO NOT HAVE A PROBLEM

So many people actually believe they need a problem so that they have something to work on or something to do. When you think this, then you must always create a problem for yourself. If this is the case, then you will go from one problem to the next. You will never have peace. Something else will always be there to replace the problem you just solved. It's like a never-ending creation of pain. It's ok to be happy. It's ok to be content. It's ok to not have a problem to work on. Recite this all day if this applies to you. "It's not a problem to not have a problem."

NOTES:

_____

_____

_____

_____

_____

_____

IT'S OK FOR YOU TO LOVE YOUR LIFE

How often are people ready to put down anyone who truly loves their life, and who have things going really well for them? How often are people ready to say those happy people don't deserve their happiness or haven't earned it? Why instead, aren't people clamoring to ask, "How do I do that? How can I love my life?" Is it time to lead the charge? Are you willing to love your life so much that people will judge you and say you didn't earn it? Are you willing to no longer make those jaded people right? It's ok to love your life. Go ahead. The judgment won't kill you, and you'll create more for the world. It's ok. The haters are going to hate. Don't let them stop you.

NOTES:

_____

_____

_____

_____

_____

_____

I WISH YOU HAPPINESS AND KINDNESS

Whenever you encounter someone, wish for them happiness and kindness. If you do this with every single person you meet, you cannot be in judgment of them. You cannot believe they don't deserve it. You cannot curse them, wish them ill, or be in a state of revenge. Doing this will then bless you and your life with happiness and kindness. Think of it: if a person is being mean or cruel, wishing them happiness and kindness might make the difference to them changing. Wishing an eye for an eye will only fortify their reasons for being cruel in the first place. "I wish you happiness and kindness." This statement will never create less in your life.

NOTES:

_____

_____

_____

_____

_____

_____

JEALOUSY

Jealousy is one of two things. Either it is program running in the mind designed to make you blame others for what they have and you don't, or it is an indication of what you wish to have, but have not yet created. A program running in the mind is designed to ensure you never decide to create on your own. It keeps you locked in a loop of wishing for it, and blaming others for having it, or making them wrong that they have it. Would you be willing to destroy every jealousy program you have ever taken in or on, known or unknown, throughout all space, time, dimension and reality? Choose that. Just ask and demand that they be destroyed and they will. And, next time you feel jealous affirm, "Oh, I desire that too. I'm having that! What will it take for me to create that?"

NOTES:

_____

_____

_____

_____

_____

JOYFUL BEING

What does it mean to be a joyful being? A joyful being is one that is not upset with the world. It's one that allows joy to be their primary operating state and one that trusts the friendly Universe we live in. It is one that lets go of everything and surrenders to the next moment. A joyful being is happy for who they are as they are. How much of a joyful being can you be today?

NOTES:

_____

_____

_____

_____

_____

_____

_____

_____

_____

JOY IS A SIGN OF THE DIVINE

What brings you joy, brings you pleasure. Often we believe pleasure is sinful. It is not. It is divine, and holy, and creates a more joyful, pleasurable world. Please let go of any notion that says your pleasure is forbidden or an abomination against God. It is an abomination against God to deny your joy. Denying your joy is the work of darkness, not light. Allow joy and pleasure today, without any guilt of wrongdoing. And enjoy!

NOTES:

_____

_____

_____

_____

_____

_____

_____

_____

_____

JOY OF CHANGE

Change brings a breath of fresh air, a new perspective, a little something different. It breaks the monotony and the tedium we live in. Change is a beautiful thing because it allows for growth, learning, curiosity, and wonder. Change brings with it the unknown to explore. It creates adventure. How much change can you now allow for that you weren't before, because you had decided change was bad? Be willing to experience and acknowledge the joy of change now.

NOTES:

JUST BE YOURSELF

There is no better way to start the day than to just be yourself. You are not lacking. You are not stupid. You are not wrong. You are not inferior; and, you are not broken. You are complete, whole, and amazing in every way. Be you. Laugh at the things you think are wrong, and you will see they don't matter. You are a unique gift to this world. Now is the time to give it. How do you do that? Just be yourself.

NOTES:

_____

_____

_____

_____

_____

_____

_____

_____

_____

JUSTICE

Justice will be done in accordance with the Laws of the Universe. Do not take justice into your own hands. Surrender it. It is not for you to decide what is right and wrong, nor is it for you to enforce punishment. Doing so only punishes you in the long run. Know all is well and being taken care of. Just focus on moving forward with joy. All else is done. Open your heart and breathe.

NOTES:

_____

_____

_____

_____

_____

_____

_____

_____

_____

KEEP ON BELIEVING

Everyone goes through tough times and down spots, and has struggles. Just keep moving. Don't stop and focus on the crap you're in. Keep focused on the bright future ahead. Keep focused on getting out of that crap as fast as possible, even if you have no idea how that might come or when that will be. Keep on trucking. Keep on believing this crap is not your destiny...because it totally is not.

NOTES:

_____

_____

_____

_____

_____

_____

_____

_____

_____

KEEP THE FAITH

It is easy to lose faith and spiral downward when things aren't going well. This is the time when we must keep looking to where we are going, which is up, instead of where we have been or are. Find a pinpoint of light in your future and focus on it until it grows. Keep affirming that "this too shall pass". Do not succumb to the lower energies that tell you things aren't getting better, and that you are doing something wrong. Refuse to go there. Instead, keep the faith.

NOTES:

_____

_____

_____

_____

_____

_____

_____

_____

_____

_____

KIND VERSUS NICE

There are many people out there who try very hard to be nice. Nice has an energy of giving to others and not receiving anything in return. The person being nice becomes the doormat. Kind has an energy that gifts to others and allows the giver to receive at the same time. True kindness is not only kind to others, but also kind to the person extending the kindness. Giving and receiving in its pure divine form happens simultaneously without strings attached, contributing to both parties. How kind can you be to yourself today by no longer needing to be nice?

NOTES:

_____

_____

_____

_____

_____

_____

_____

LAUGH IN THE FACE OF ADVERSITY

Laughter is the most healing energy on the planet. A true laugh will dispel darkness, make demons flee, and bring joy to you and those around you. Whatever may be troubling you, whatever may be causing you to take life seriously or believe adversity is serious business - laugh. Laugh at it. Laugh with it. Laugh despite it. Laugh because it is a choice you always have.

NOTES:

_____

_____

_____

_____

_____

_____

_____

_____

_____

LAUGHS AND GIGGLES

A laugh can stimulate the immune system for 24 hours and an upset or angry moment can suppress your immune system for 48 hours. Is it time to make it a priority to focus on the humor in life? Is it time to give up working on problems and getting serious about life, which only leads to illness and a suppressed immune system? What's more fun anyway? Ha Ha! Time for a laugh. Come on. Right out loud – right now. Laugh.

NOTES:

_____

_____

_____

_____

_____

_____

_____

_____

LEAP OF FAITH

To get a different result, you have to do or be something that you've never done or been before. This requires a leap of faith. Sometimes we must trust that a risk isn't going to kill us or ruin us - because really it isn't. Fear usually accompanies great change. It doesn't make the change wrong. Trust your knowing. You have a knowing whether something will create more for you or whether it will go down badly. If you are wishing you could just jump with ease, then jump. It is the wishing that you could jump that lets you know it's the right move for you.

NOTES:

_____

_____

_____

_____

_____

_____

_____

LET GO OF YOUR REASONS

You will have good reasons as to why you are grumpy, mad, upset, sad, or depressed. What if you let go of them? What if you didn't make any of those things important? Instead, what if you chose without reasons? What if you chose joy for no reason at all? What if it is your reasons keeping you from the thing you truly desire - to just be? Will you let go of the reasons that keep you from joy or just being, and allow yourself peace and contentment instead?

NOTES:

_____

_____

_____

_____

_____

_____

_____

_____

_____

LET'S GET IT DONE; LET'S HAVE SOME FUN

The two are not mutually exclusive. Both can happen at the same time. If you combine fun with getting it done, it often gets done faster and with higher quality. Whatever you've been avoiding, get it done while having some fun. Wherever you've been putting your nose to the grindstone, have some fun while getting it done.

NOTES:

_____

_____

_____

_____

_____

_____

_____

_____

LET YOUR PAST GO

Your past has nothing to do with your future...or even your present, unless you drag it forward. Move on from it. What is one thing from your past you bring with you that you can now say, "I'm leaving you here, and moving along without you? Thank you for riding with me. This is your stop." Now, drive away. Go while looking forward, knowing you are heading to something greater and more desirable for you and your life.

NOTES:

_____

_____

_____

_____

_____

_____

_____

_____

_____

_____

LIFE IS GRAND

Life is grand. From it springs forth endless creation. Life is joyous and abundant. Life is adventurous and exciting. When we choose to really live, we experience all that life has to offer. Are you choosing to really live? What would change if you did?

NOTES:

_____

_____

_____

_____

_____

_____

_____

_____

_____

_____

LISTENING WITH YOUR HEART

Trust the messages you receive from your heart. It is the heart and not the head that knows what is best for you and will bring you the greatest joys. Listen to it. What joy might you encounter if you allowed your heart to open? What wonders might you discover when you let your heart move you? Let your heart be the guiding voice, not the head, today and everyday.

NOTES:

_____

_____

_____

_____

_____

_____

_____

_____

_____

LISTEN TO THAT CRAZY VOICE

Whenever you have a crazy idea pop in out of the blue, you may want to listen to it. It is often our head that talks us out of listening, saying that the moment of clarity is craziness. Then, we don't act upon it. For example, once in the middle of the night I popped out of bed, and with a mad scramble went out onto our balcony and brought in all the clothes that were drying out there. I didn't know why I was bothering. I was just listening to a crazy voice I couldn't ignore. A few minutes later, it was pouring rain. Don't get soaked by ignoring your crazy voice. It's so crazy, it's sane.

NOTES:

_____

_____

_____

_____

_____

_____

_____

LONG TIME FRIENDS

Long time friends are those people who know us at our best, our worst, and our most embarrassing. They know our stupidity and our brilliance. They like us for who we are no matter what we have done. I wonder what it would take for you to treat yourself like a long time friend - with kindness, forgiveness, allowance, and irreverence? I wonder what it would take for you to be your longest and best friend, who keeps inspiring and supporting you no matter what? I mean, who has known you and stuck with you the longest? Isn't it you?

NOTES:

_____

_____

_____

_____

_____

_____

_____

_____

LOOKING DEEPER

Everything you need is within you - no matter how deep you've buried it. Stop trying to find answers outside yourself. Everything you need to know is within you. Look deeper inside yourself. What do you know? What truly do you desire? What choices do you truly have? Are you willing to make them? Look deeper today, and find the truth within. Remember, it is all there.

NOTES:

_____

_____

_____

_____

_____

_____

_____

_____

LOOSEN YOUR PURSE STRINGS

Just loosen. You don't have to open your purse up wide and dump it all out. When we believe that there is not enough and that times are tight, we automatically tighten the purse strings. We hoard. This is akin to telling the Universe, "There's not enough. I must save what I have because there isn't more coming." The Universe matches your energy exactly and makes life so that there is the feeling of not enough and with no more coming. Loosen the purse strings and let the Universe know that you know there is always more, there is always enough, and you are generously provided for. Then, the Universe will match exactly that.

NOTES:

_____

_____

_____

_____

_____

_____

_____

_____

LOVE YOUR BODY

Often we want to change our body because we hate it. What if we wanted to change our body because we loved it? What if we acted out of love instead of hate? What might that create? When we hate our body, we put out an energy to the Universe that is matched exactly, which then creates more to hate about our body. When we love our body, that energy is matched, and we get more to love about our body. Is it time to stop being mean to your body, and start loving it?

NOTES:

_____

_____

_____

_____

_____

_____

_____

_____

MAGIC

Magic happens when you are open to the possibilities of what something may become, and not when you are determined to control something into being the way you want it. What possibilities are you ignoring in order to keep your life under control? What magic are you truly capable of creating that you are not acknowledging? You are magic. Anything you allow will come to you. Let go of control and open to receive.

NOTES:

_____

_____

_____

_____

_____

_____

_____

_____

_____

MAGIC IS NOT PREDICTABLE

Have you ever noticed that the magic in your life comes in a way that you could never imagine? Stop trying to figure out how something will or must come to be. The Universe does a much better and easier job of doing that. Keep focused on what you desire without ever doubting its arrival. How it shows up is always a lovely surprise, and usually more brilliant than you can imagine.

NOTES:

_____

_____

_____

_____

_____

_____

_____

_____

MAKE LEMONADE

"When life gives you lemons, make lemonade." There is much wisdom in this old phrase. How often do we stew about our lemons and make them wrong? When something happens that isn't to your liking or expectation, don't automatically decide something is going wrong. Instead, ask, "How is this benefitting me?" What if everything we received was a contribution to our lives? Too often we totally miss the point, because we are too busy judging it. What can you make lemonade from today that you are certain is just a crappy lemon?

NOTES:

_____

_____

_____

_____

_____

_____

_____

MAKE TODAY YOUR DAY

How often do you include yourself - your wishes, your joy, and your fun - into your day? Make today that day and every day after that. Put you into your day. Put you into your life. When your energy is present and accounted for, you will feel like you are taken into consideration, and things will be much more pleasant and enjoyable. Make today your day!

NOTES:

_____

_____

_____

_____

_____

_____

_____

_____

_____

_____

MIRACLES HAPPEN EVERYDAY TO YOU

Everyday. Have you noticed? Let's start counting. When you begin to acknowledge and be grateful for miracles everyday in your life, the Universe matches that energy and brings it back to you. What does that mean? More miracles. Everyday.

NOTES:

_____

_____

_____

_____

_____

_____

_____

_____

_____

_____

MOVING FORWARD FEARLESSLY

Sometimes you like to put up little roadblocks to stop you from moving forward. It is time to go around them or blast them out of the way, because they are not based in any truth. No matter what your goal or wish is, keep moving toward it, even when you think you can't. Just keep going! Eventually, you will find what you thought was difficult is easier than you thought. Keep moving forward fearlessly today and everyday. Why? Because you can.

NOTES:

_____

_____

_____

_____

_____

_____

_____

_____

_____

NOBODY LIKES ME

Many of us are walking around with this as a core belief. The problem with it (other than it being a total lie) is that most people don't realize that nobody includes them. If you believe no one likes you, then you cannot like yourself. Will you allow this lie to unravel by acknowledging how very much you do like you? You are liked. I like you. Damn, doesn't it just piss you off when you find out you're wrong about something you've held onto as true for so many years? I like that about you.

NOTES:

_____

_____

_____

_____

_____

_____

_____

_____

NURTURE

How often do you take time to nurture your spirit, your body, or your life? What would it take to make that a priority for you? Why not take time out of today for you - whether it be a walk in nature, a massage, meditation, laughing with friends, or doing something you love? When you nurture something, it grows and blossoms. Is it time to do that for you?

NOTES:

_____

_____

_____

_____

_____

_____

_____

_____

_____

_____

PAIN

Pain is often a message that we are refusing to listen to. Instead of resisting pain by trying to make it go away, why not do something completely different? Try talking to it and asking it what message it has for you. Then, listen - not for words - but for awareness. Let down your guard and belief that the pain is out to get you, and let it tell you what it is desperately trying to get you to pay attention to. You might even find out it was never yours.

NOTES:

_____

_____

_____

_____

_____

_____

_____

_____

PERSONAL SAVIORS

The problem with needing to have a personal savior is that it makes you believe that you need saving. What do you need saving from? What if you are completely self-reliant? While others will always be there to help and aid you in having fun on your journey, what if you don't need someone to fix you? Or to judge you? What if you're not broken? Or wrong? Drop the notion that you need saving or that you need to save others. How much more fun could you have if you did?

NOTES:

PLAY OR PUSH

Are you playful with life? Do you look at the possibilities you can create and wonder with glee what you might be able to make happen? Are you grateful to play with the Universal magic that is always available to you? Or does life seemingly push you around? Are you pushing too hard, always trying to control things into being or to force an outcome? Pushing takes effort and isn't so fun. Lighten up and go at life from a sense of play and wonder. You may just find that life is worth living.

NOTES:

_____

_____

_____

_____

_____

_____

_____

_____

PROGRESS

Sometimes it is beneficial to take stock of how far you have come - especially when you think nothing is changing. How different are you today from 5 years ago? Has anything changed? Imagine how different your life might be in 5 years time? You are progressing - probably faster than you are willing to admit. Keep going, and don't forget to give yourself a pat on the back.

NOTES:

_____

_____

_____

_____

_____

_____

_____

_____

_____

PROTECTION

When we decide that something or someone needs protection, we must create them/it as weak or create a circumstance to put them/it in danger, so that we can then protect them/it. How many victims do we create by trying to be protectors? What if we all were perfectly safe and did not require protection? What if we saw everyone as capable and strong? What protection might that create?

NOTES:

_____

_____

_____

_____

_____

_____

_____

_____

RECEIVE YOUR INTUITIVE GUIDANCE THE EASIEST WAY FOR YOU

Often people are looking for their intuitive guidance in the hardest way possible. They try to hear messages when really they feel the truth; or they try to see the sign when really they know what it is. What is easiest for you? Is it hearing, seeing, tasting, smelling, feeling, or knowing? Connect back to what is easiest for you, and you will always have the guidance you require. It's with you 24/7.

NOTES:

_____

_____

_____

_____

_____

_____

_____

_____

RECEIVING HELP

Real help is kind. Real help empowers you. Often we are offered "help" that says, "You're not capable. Let me do that for you." Or "I know what's better for you than you do." This isn't real help. Real help will always empower and uplift you. Don't close yourself off to real help just because a few losers tried to disempower you with their version of help. Recognize the difference, and be willing to let down your guard when it really will contribute to you. Allow yourself to receive help again. You no longer have to do everything yourself. You are not in this alone, and there is real help that is kind to you. Ask for it and receive it; and, say no to the false help that puts you down.

NOTES:

_____

_____

_____

_____

_____

_____

_____

RELAX

Do you ever have your head going a million miles a minute and feel like you are moving on hyper-drive? If so, that means you are running on adrenaline. That is very tough on your body and can often make it hard to sleep at night. Breathe. Take a moment and relax. Slow down and get present. Ask your body to stop using adrenaline and to come back into balance and calm. Often this is just enough to get the body to relax and allow you to move productively throughout your day. You will also sleep better at night.

NOTES:

_____

_____

_____

_____

_____

_____

_____

_____

RELEASING RESISTANCE

How much resistance do you use against you? Close your eyes and become aware of everything you are resisting. Now, allow yourself to no longer resist it. Give up. Surrender. Relax. Allow. Receive. You are safe. You are whole. You are supported in this. It is time to stop resisting the wonder of you and of this world and start receiving it. The world won't fall apart. It will fall together. Release your resistance now. If you can't, then release your resistance to the resistance.

NOTES:

_____

_____

_____

_____

_____

_____

_____

_____

_____

RENEWING YOUR LIFE

Let go of the old and bring in the new. Reduce clutter, clean, and refresh your environment, your thoughts, and your soul. Renew whatever requires attention. Bring luster to what is dull in your life. Refresh yourself. Revive your life with a little gusto! Put polish on what is tarnished. Clear away dust and cobwebs. Now is the time to let go of the old to bring in a glorious new! Enjoy!

NOTES:

_____

_____

_____

_____

_____

_____

_____

_____

_____

SADNESS IS A CHOICE

Most people don't realize sadness is a choice. It is not a wrong choice and it is not a right choice. It is just a choice. So is happiness. Take ownership of your choice without judgment. If you wish to be sad, be sad. If you wish to be happy, be happy. Be whatever you choose to be, but not for one second believe you have no other choice. You do. You just aren't allowing yourself to choose it, or you are judging yourself for the choice you have made.

NOTES:

_____

_____

_____

_____

_____

_____

_____

_____

_____

_____

SAY YES

We spend our lives saying no to many things. What would you like to say yes to? Would you say YES to living joyfully? Would you say YES to abundance? Would you say YES to change? Open to receive the YES and know you will need to let go of a few NO's in order to do so. What can you say yes to right now that would immediately change your life for the better?

NOTES:

_____

_____

_____

_____

_____

_____

_____

_____

_____

SEE ANOTHER'S POINT OF VIEW

We often become accustomed to viewing a situation only from one angle - our own. This does not allow for understanding and compassion of other viewpoints. When we see a situation from another's eyes, by standing in their shoes, we begin to notice that the world is not as black and white as we may think. We begin to notice that people are doing the best that they can with the tools and knowledge they have. We begin to notice that there are many sides to a situation, and that we are not completely 'right' about it, because we truly do not have the whole picture. When you see someone behaving what you might call badly today, step back and see life through their eyes. You may find that instead of your judgment they could use your love, your support, or your help. Instead of finding yourself in a state of ridicule, you will find yourself in a state of compassion and acting with kindness. This will make for a better day. I promise.

NOTES:

_____

_____

_____

_____

SEE WHERE YOU'RE GOING, NOT WHERE YOU'VE BEEN

When you keep focusing on where you've been, you keep reliving and recreating the past. It is time to focus solely on where you are going. Never take your eyes off of that. Never look back! There is no need to. You've already been there, done that. Relax and focus on where you are going. Trust you will be guided all the way there with ease and joy.

NOTES:

_____

_____

_____

_____

_____

_____

_____

_____

SELF-RELIANCE

You can count on yourself because you have all the answers and resources you need within you. Sometimes those answers and resources will involve other people, but do not be fooled. You are the creator of your own life, and everything you need comes from a vibration within you. Believe in yourself and your abilities. Also, listen to the wise inner voice of your heart and soul. Sometimes we wish to listen to the advice of others, but the truth lies within. Trust yourself and act on what is best for you. When you do that, in the long run, it will be what is best for everyone else too.

NOTES:

_____

_____

_____

_____

_____

_____

_____

SERIOUSLY, LIGHTEN UP!

You cannot create with ease by getting serious about your issue or your desire. You must find a way to lighten up about it. Light energy is fast, quick, and easy. Serious energy is heavy, slow, and hard. Go against your go-to response of seriousness and be playful, joyful, carefree, and silly about things. Lighten up and your world will lighten up with it. Sometimes you just have to laugh at how much of a grumpy pants you can be and at how important you like making little things.

NOTES:

_____

_____

_____

_____

_____

_____

_____

_____

SHOWER OF ABUNDANCE

The Universe is constantly showering abundance upon you. Will you open to receive it? Or will you continue to decide that you don't deserve it, that it must be meant for someone else, or that you can go without? Is it time to open all pockets, nooks, and crannies and let the shower of abundance cleanse and restore all those neglected areas? Open to receive.

NOTES:

_____

_____

_____

_____

_____

_____

_____

_____

_____

_____

SIGNIFICANCE

Everything we make significant in our lives will become an issue. In order to release the issues of our lives, we must then release the significance we have put to them. For example, if you berate yourself for having a one-night stand, for shoplifting, or for being mean to someone, it is because you made doing those things significant. If it is no longer significant, you can make another choice. You can stop judging you. You can look at things objectively and decide whether or not you wish to continue choosing what you chose, without punishing yourself and without feeling guilty. Make everything less significant and you can have a lot more joy and ease in your life.

NOTES:

SILLY

How silly do you allow yourself to be? Do you have a belief that being silly is stupid and that being serious is smart? Is it? Which one brings more lightness and fun into your world? Would you be willing to give up being serious for silly and realize that you have been stupid thinking being serious is smart? I wonder what a difference that might make in your world if you did?

NOTES:

_____

_____

_____

_____

_____

_____

_____

_____

_____

SINGING AND DANCING

Express yourself and allow yourself the magic that happens with music and movement. Feeling stuck? Move your body - using dancing or some other method. Feeling blue? Sing. Use music to shift your mood. Play or sing happy music. Sometimes all that is required to create change is to change what you normally do. So get moving. Get singing. Get happy!

NOTES:

_____

_____

_____

_____

_____

_____

_____

_____

_____

SLOW DOWN

When you feel yourself going a million miles a minute and not in a good way, slow down. There is enough time for everything. Enjoy the journey. This doesn't mean you can't move quickly. It means you become present in the moments that are moving quickly. Presence defies time. So slow down, become present, then move like the super-wizard that you are!!!

NOTES:

_____

_____

_____

_____

_____

_____

_____

_____

SNAP OUT OF IT

We can easily get into a trance, a funk, a belief, or some other crap that makes us believe we can not overcome or get out of our circumstances. SNAP OUT OF IT! You are an infinite being and a powerful creator. Why let small, insignificant things stop you? Because you have made them big and significant? SNAP OUT OF IT! What do you wish to choose? Choose it, and don't let any reason be significant. Don't allow any one thing or situation matter to where you are headed or what you are choosing.

NOTES:

_____

_____

_____

_____

_____

_____

_____

_____

SOARING INTO JOY

In order to soar into joy allow a little childlike wonder into your life. Children are not weighted down with doubts and cynicism, so they are generally much more joyful than adults. They laugh and play and believe in the magic of the Universe. This is a perfect time to ignite the childlike magic within. Believe in something beautiful. Believe in the magic of miracles. Soar into the possibility of laughter and carefree joy! Like a balloon that is weighted down, understand you must cut that tether in order to fly into the air and soar! Feel lighter today. Feel joyful today. If you have no reason to feel joyful, then, feel joyful for no reason at all!

NOTES:

_____

_____

_____

_____

_____

_____

_____

SPIRIT GUIDES

True divine spirit guides offer unconditional guidance. Sometimes we think we need guidance to show us right from wrong, and we hire a "guide" to do that. This is not a high level, unconditional loving guide. If you have done this or have a guide (a voice in your head) that punishes you, fire it. Send it away forever. Ask that you be guided only by beings of true consciousness, which are ones that will love you unconditionally and guide you without judgment. Otherwise you are not being guided. You are being controlled, punished and judged.

NOTES:

_____

_____

_____

_____

_____

_____

_____

STANDING FIRM

Stand firm in your decisions to move forward and create change. Stand firm in your decision to reap joy out of this day. Stand firm in the knowingness that more is possible than this reality says. Stand firm in your conviction to create the magic you know is there for you. Don't let anyone or anything bring you down. You are a powerhouse. You are an amazing being. Remember that. Stand firm in your resolve today. You can and you will.

NOTES:

_____

_____

_____

_____

_____

_____

_____

_____

_____

_____

START OFF YOUR DAY WITH INTENTION

Sometimes we have to take matters into our own hands - like creating a life we love. Why not choose to start off each day purposely demanding the joy, beauty, and abundance this day has to offer? Why not choose to focus on gratitude and possibility in the morning instead of rehashing the drudgery of yesterday and thinking today is going to be the same? What does this day have to offer that you aren't choosing? Go looking for it. If you do, your day will be better. I promise.

NOTES:

_____

_____

_____

_____

_____

_____

_____

_____

STOP TORTURING YOURSELF

Do you torture yourself? Do you put yourself into worry, blame, or upset? Do you belittle you and bring yourself down? What do you love about torturing yourself? Is torturing yourself somehow seemingly the right thing to do? Will you stop? Will you choose something else, and no longer be victim of your own doing? The world is not becoming a better place by you torturing yourself, just as you are not becoming a better person because of it either. It's time to stop this madness. Nurture yourself instead.

NOTES:

_____

_____

_____

_____

_____

_____

_____

_____

STRETCH

Have you ever noticed the first thing a cat or a small child does when they awaken is stretch? Physically, it is a great way to get connected back with your beautiful body that is here to take you through this life and this day. Then, there is the less literal, more metaphorical meaning of beginning the day with a stretch. "Today I will stretch myself. I will stretch past my limits, my fears, and my beliefs. Today, I stretch." How far and much can you stretch yourself and your body today?

NOTES:

_____

_____

_____

_____

_____

_____

_____

_____

_____

STUBBORN PRIDE

How much has stubborn pride helped you in your life? Or has it stopped you from choosing anything else? Stubborn pride is like the ultimate state of righteousness - we dig in our heels, and, under no circumstances, do we budge. How often do we ask, "Would it be worthwhile to budge?" Even if the answer is yes, stubborn pride won't allow for it. Is it time to use stubborn pride against itself and decide that, no matter what, it is time to move, change, and at the very least, budge from your entrenched position? Stubborn pride says, "You'll lose." The truth is, however, by losing your position, you win, because now you can move on.

NOTES:

_____

_____

_____

_____

_____

_____

_____

SUPPORT

Are you supporting you or are you fighting against those that don't support you? If you wish for support, your primary energy has to be focused upon it, and not on destroying the absence of it. Let go of the fight to destroy non-support. Instead, focus on supporting you and others, leaving the naysayers to their own fight. They will not hurt you.

NOTES:

_____

_____

_____

_____

_____

_____

_____

_____

_____

_____

SYNCHRONICITY

Your prayers and petitions are being answered through signs and synchronistic events – so pay attention! We have to be aware of the information we are being given and follow them with total faith. When we do this, we always are blessed. Know that what you need may be only one meeting away or one moment away. Look for synchronicities today. Watch for the signs and follow them with complete faith, knowing you are always divinely guided.

NOTES:

_____

_____

_____

_____

_____

_____

_____

_____

_____

TAKE OFF YOUR GRUMPY PANTS

Ever get annoyed at something, then, everything seems to annoy you? It's like you start collecting annoyances. That's because grumpy pants have big pockets. Instead, put on your blessings blue jeans. The pockets are just as big, if not bigger. But it takes a firm decision to do this. It takes determination to no longer wear those grumpy pants, especially when every one else is. Be a trendsetter, and wear some new blessings blue jeans.

NOTES:

_____

_____

_____

_____

_____

_____

_____

_____

_____

TAKING ACTION

Enthusiastically embrace life's boundless possibilities! What can you choose that when you choose it will bring you joy - not comfort – but joy? Take action on that. Take a risk and take action – now – not tomorrow, not next week, now! Make something happen in your life. Make life new. When you create the same ol' same ol', you never grow and you never feel the excitement newness and creation creates. Jump out of the comfort zone and take action now!

NOTES:

_____

_____

_____

_____

_____

_____

_____

_____

_____

THE DIFFERENCE OF YOU

Many of us have a knowing that we are different. Many of us have erroneously decided that being different is wrong. What if it is not? What if it is the key to us feeling as though we fit in? What if acknowledging how different we are, and allowing for that difference will take away that feeling of being out of place? We've tried to fit in for too long without success. Is it time to try something else...like being who we are, which is different?

NOTES:

_____

_____

_____

_____

_____

_____

_____

_____

THE ONLY THING TO FEAR IS FEAR ITSELF

And even then, is it even necessary to fear fear? What would it be like if you stopped being afraid of fear? It hasn't killed you yet, and it never will, because it is nothing. Fear is not real. It is an illusion created to keep us captive and limit ourselves. When we face "fear", we always conquer, because fear has no real power. It has the illusion of power when we won't face it. Face it. You're fearless and fear is nothing but a distraction to you being as magnificent as you truly are.

NOTES:

_____

_____

_____

_____

_____

_____

_____

_____

THERE'S NOTHING TO WORRY ABOUT

Let all your troubles and worries go. There is nothing to worry about. Surrender any fears and give your mind a rest. You don't have to figure this out. If you could have you would have already. Stop thinking and start surrendering. There is nothing to worry about, so don't give it another thought. Instead, focus on the gratitude that all is well and is working out in perfect order - because it is. So let it. There is nothing to worry about.

NOTES:

_____

_____

_____

_____

_____

_____

_____

_____

_____

THE UNIVERSE ALWAYS CONTRIBUTES

The Universe always gives. It is not working against you. When something happens that you judge as bad, take a moment to acknowledge that the Universe is always contributing to you. Ask, "How is this a gift? How is this NOT a problem? How can I create something greater from this or beyond this?" When you realize nothing is against you, you start creating your life from the vantage point of totally being supported. Keep in mind, no matter what, the Universe is always contributing to you - even though you may not comprehend how.

NOTES:

_____

_____

_____

_____

_____

_____

_____

THE WORST IS OVER

Each day will get better and better if you let it. Open to receive it. Things will only get worse if you are not finished with hurting yourself, hating yourself, needing to prove you are right about how horrible things are for you, or needing to prove how horrible someone else is to you or others. Let go of needing that. Choose for today to be better. Refuse to accept anything else.

NOTES:

_____

_____

_____

_____

_____

_____

_____

_____

_____

THIS TOO SHALL PASS

I love this phrase and it reminds me never to get too bogged down in seriousness or worry. All seemingly "bad" things happening in life are temporary, and can blossom into something beautiful or dissolve into thin air. This too shall pass and tomorrow is another day. Whatever weighs heavy in your heart, know that it is not here forever. This too shall pass. You can allow your heart to lighten.

NOTES:

_____

_____

_____

_____

_____

_____

_____

_____

TIME IS MADE FOR WHAT YOU CHOOSE

Have you ever noticed this? When you choose something, somehow the time to do it appears. When you choose to go to the gym no matter what, the time to do it appears. When you choose to go on vacation, the time for it appears. When you choose to be a workaholic, the time to work appears. What can you choose that when you choose it, the time for it would appear?

NOTES:

_____

_____

_____

_____

_____

_____

_____

_____

TRUE POWER

Many of us are using the wrong definition of power. We erroneously believe power lies in the ability to be violent, cruel, or controlling. That is not power. True power is light, strong, pure, and confident. It is sure of itself. It will always outsmart the brutal hands of force and cruelty. Open to your true power today and know that you are not weak in your kindness, awareness, and lightness.

NOTES:

_____

_____

_____

_____

_____

_____

_____

_____

TRUST IN YOU

Trust is not that people will do the right thing or the thing that honors you. That's blind faith and if you aren't using your awareness, can let you down again and again. Trust is trusting that people will choose as they have chosen before. This includes you. You might be able to trust that you will always have a messy desk, or that you will speed on long road trips. You might trust that you will try to sabotage a relationship or lie to your parents. There is no right or wrong in this. When you work from trust, you begin to trust yourself to be who you are and recognize the choices you are making. This spills over in allowing others to be who they are, and to recognize the choices they are making. Blind faith that you will have a clean desktop will only make you upset when you don't. So trust, in you and in others, without judgment, and choose from there.

NOTES:

_____

_____

_____

_____

_____

TRUST THE UNIVERSE

If you totally trusted in the Universe to have your back, how much could you relax? Allow yourself to breathe and melt into the beauty and kindness that the Universe has for you. Receive it. Let down your guard and allow the Universe to catch you. Allow it to give to you. Allow it to be acknowledged for the kind, generous, appreciative beast that it is.

NOTES:

_____

_____

_____

_____

_____

_____

_____

_____

_____

UNIVERSE, SHOW ME SOMETHING MAGICAL TODAY

This phrase never ceases to disappoint. The Universe is magical and willing to show you when asked. Have you asked? Go ahead. Put in your request - not with cynicism or doubt, but a true request spoken with childlike wonder. "Universe, show me something magical today." I wonder might show up?

NOTES:

_____

_____

_____

_____

_____

_____

_____

_____

_____

_____

VENDETTA

Who are you trying to make hurt as much as they hurt you? Is it working? Or are you just hurting more? We must give up all our need or desire for revenge in order to truly be done with an issue. Justice isn't the same thing as healing. An eye for an eye just creates more pain and blindness in the world. It creates a cycle of revenge. Letting go means releasing all judgment and blame. Just be done with it. Not for their sake, but for yours. That's true justice, because it means you won't suffer any longer.

NOTES:

_____

_____

_____

_____

_____

_____

_____

_____

WAKE UP AND SMELL THE COFFEE

What is the first thing you think of when you awaken? Is it to go back to sleep? Is it "Oh crap, it's morning."? Why not train yourself to drink in life when you wake up? What can you enjoy upon awakening? Is it the anticipation of smelling brewed coffee? The joy of what magic the day may bring? Is it the gratitude you have for this day, and what you may do with it? Perhaps there are other options available that you have not been considering. What might your day be like if you woke up and blissfully smelled the coffee?

NOTES:

_____

_____

_____

_____

_____

_____

_____

WHAT A DIFFERENCE A DAY MAKES

Ever have one of those days where you don't feel like yourself and everything seems to be going off the rails? If you can just remind yourself that it is just "one of those days", stop judging yourself for it, and know that tomorrow is another day, you will survive it much better. Sometimes you just need to sit with crap before you make your next move so that when you do, you don't create more crap. Remember, what a difference a day makes.

NOTES:

_____

_____

_____

_____

_____

_____

_____

_____

_____

WHAT AM I DOING WRONG?

We often ask this question when things aren't going our way. We automatically put ourselves at fault and search frantically for the answer. Asking what you are doing wrong will always create more "wrong", because you need to figure it out. You get more "wrong" because you are analyzing what you are doing to make it so. That's not solution. Solution is demanding that it changes. Choose to put your energy into changing it. You don't need to know how. You just need to decide that it is happening. And, then, it will.

NOTES:

_____

_____

_____

_____

_____

_____

_____

_____

WHAT AREN'T YOU INCLUDING?

We live in an inclusive Universe, yet most of us are trying to exclude what we don't want thinking that will be an infinitely better choice. It is not. Instead of trying to get rid of the unwanted, ask what it is you need to add or include in your world to make it better. If you have sadness, you might need to add joy – not subtract sadness. If you have conflict, harmony may be required. Do like the infinite Universe does: include and never exclude.

NOTES:

_____

_____

_____

_____

_____

_____

_____

_____

WHAT ARE YOU COMMITTED TO?

Are you committed to joy and laughter? Are you committed to fun and ease? Or, are you committed to hard work and struggle? Complaint and worry? Sometimes we have to let go of some of our commitments in order for things to change. Sometimes we have to commit to the things that seem elusive to bring them into being. What are you committed to? Are you willing to be less committed to some of it?

NOTES:

_____

_____

_____

_____

_____

_____

_____

_____

_____

WHAT ARE YOU FIGHTING AGAINST?

We often believe that if we fight against what we don't like, then it will change or be destroyed. Not so. Energetically the Universe matches the energy you put out. If you fight against something, then the Universe will provide you with more of the very thing you are fighting against, so that you can continue to fight it. You actually are creating more of the problem you wish to solve. Stop fighting and start focusing on things being as you wish they would be. Want to end animal abuse? Then focus on the loving, kind treatment of animals - and the universe will match it and have to create more of that. Want your spouse to stop doing something? Focus on the things that they do that you appreciate and stop making him/her wrong. Is it time to stop fighting, so that the Universe knows your war is over and can give you peace?

NOTES:

_____

_____

_____

_____

_____

_____

WHAT ARE YOU REFUSING?

Are you refusing to have a good time, an easy life, or a happy day? Are you convinced it is all working against you, not going your way, and happening to you and not by you? What if you stopped needing to prove life is tough? What would you have to change? What would you have to stop refusing? A smile and a laugh are right there within you. You just have to stop refusing to let them out.

NOTES:

_____

_____

_____

_____

_____

_____

_____

_____

_____

WHAT ENERGY ARE YOU BEING?

This is one of my favorite questions, because the energy that we are being is exactly what we will create in the future. Are you worried? Then, you are putting in an order to create circumstances that will continue to make you worry. Are you annoyed? Then, you are putting in an order to create more things to annoy you. Sometimes, in our pursuit of happiness, it is nice to stop and just be happy. Could you be the energy of happy, or grateful, or kind? Then you will be creating more of that in the future. What energy are you being? If it doesn't suit you, please know you have a choice to be something else.

NOTES:

_____

_____

_____

_____

_____

_____

WHAT GIVES YOU A THRILL?

What gives you butterflies in your stomach or makes you feel like a little kid at the fair? What excites you? Do that. Create with that. Create that for you. Do something that seems a little crazy, or out of your comfort zone, or that makes your heart race. Spoil yourself with a gift. Give yourself a thrill.

NOTES:

_____

_____

_____

_____

_____

_____

_____

_____

_____

_____

WHAT IF BEING RIGHT LIMITS YOU?

What are you right about that keeps screwing you over? When we believe we are right about something, it is hard to create past it. If you believe you are poor or middle class, it is unlikely you will become rich. If you believe that people don't like you, it is unlikely that you will ever feel truly loved and appreciated. If you believe you are a victim, it is unlikely you will ever not feel persecuted and powerless. Is it time to let go of being right about how things are for you, so that a different possibility can show up?

NOTES:

_____

_____

_____

_____

_____

_____

_____

_____

WHAT IF CHOICE IS MORE VALUABLE THAN OTHER PEOPLE'S HAPPINESS?

What if choice was the most valuable product? Often we make other people's happiness the most valuable product, which means we will give up our choice in order to make others happy. What if we celebrated someone's ability to choose instead of the choice they are choosing? Then, we would no longer need to give up our choice to be happy, to have fun, or to be ourselves, even if it makes someone else upset. We could just celebrate that someone else has chosen to be upset. Value your choices and other's choices today. You may find it brings you happiness.

NOTES:

_____

_____

_____

_____

_____

_____

_____

WHAT IF LIFE IS EASY?

We have heard it time and time again, "Life isn't easy," or "This hard life." What if it isn't true? What might you do or create differently? When we believe something, we must then create things in order to prove how right we are about that belief, so that we can make the belief true. Is it time to stop believing that life is hard? Is it time to stop making that belief true? What if life is easy?

NOTES:

_____

_____

_____

_____

_____

_____

_____

_____

_____

WHAT IF NOTHING IS WRONG WITH YOU?

Whenever we are trying to fix something about ourselves, we have determined that there is something wrong with us. What if nothing was wrong with us? What if this acknowledgement alone would "fix" the problem, because then there would be no problem? How many assumptions would you have to let go of to allow there to be nothing wrong with you? Would you let go of them? Or do you wish to continue to be right about how wrong you are? Ponder it. What if nothing is wrong with you?

NOTES:

_____

_____

_____

_____

_____

_____

_____

_____

WHAT IF YOU'RE WRONG?

You may pride yourself on being right, but there are some things you are right about that would change your life dramatically, in a good way, if you allowed yourself to be wrong. Are you sure you are right about life being hard? What if you're wrong? Are you sure you are right about needing to work hard to get ahead and that the more you struggle the more you create? What if you are totally wrong about that? Then, the truth would be that life is easy and having fun is productive. Would you be willing to be wrong about all the things you are sure you are right about in order to create an easier life? What could you be right about that would make your life easier?

NOTES:

_____

_____

_____

_____

_____

_____

_____

WHAT IF YOU STOPPED JUDGING YOU FOR THE STUFF YOU DO?

What if you stopped judging you for the choices you make and begin enjoying your choices instead? Like when you have that piece of cake. How much judgment do you impose upon yourself in order to eat it? What if you stopped? Would that be more kind to your body, or less? What if you stopped judging you for spending money, or for liking something taboo, or for doing something different? If you're going to choose it, celebrate it. Enjoy it. Never be ashamed to like or even love something - no matter what it is. No judgment. Just choice. No judgment. Just celebration for you choosing it.

NOTES:

_____

_____

_____

_____

_____

_____

_____

WHAT - NOT HOW

Are you asking for what you want or are you asking for how it can happen? Go for what you want, and let the Universe figure out how. It does it so much better and easier than you do. Trying to figure out how something will happen will only slow you down or ruin your creation altogether. Stay focused on: What do I desire? What am I having? Where am I headed?

NOTES:

_____

_____

_____

_____

_____

_____

_____

_____

_____

_____

WHAT REQUIRES YOUR ATTENTION TODAY?

Every morning, when you wake up, ask this question and be still. You will be given information about what needs your attention today. The Universe wants your day to go smoothly and easily. It wishes to work with you. It can see from a much greater perspective than you can. Trust it. What requires your attention today?

NOTES:

_____

_____

_____

_____

_____

_____

_____

_____

_____

WHAT'S FUNNY ABOUT THIS?

When you get serious about life or see no humor in your situation at all, then it is time to ask, "What's funny about this?" Everything is funny if you let it be. Laughter and joy are the greatest healers and contributors on this planet. Let's not allow anything to get in the way of that. So, what's funny about this? Really ask...and keep asking until you laugh. You may find it takes no time at all to get the joke.

NOTES:

_____

_____

_____

_____

_____

_____

_____

_____

WHAT'S NEW?

What's new? Anything? Or is it the same old stuff? Is it time to create something new? Be willing to jump out of the ordinary and do something different. Be willing to choose to have something new in your life. Is now the time to create it?

NOTES:

_____

_____

_____

_____

_____

_____

_____

_____

_____

_____

WHAT'S THE VALUE OF _____?

Anything that is recurring in our lives, we have deemed to have some sort of value (which is why we keep it). Sometimes it is enlightening to ask what the value of a choice is. What's the value of sabotaging my efforts? What's the value of constantly putting me down? What's the value of staying small? What's the value of having difficulty with money? What's the value of attracting losers in relationships? What's the value of this illness I have? And so on. When you honestly ask the question, you will see there is some value to you. Once you are aware of that, then you can choose to keep going business as usual, or no longer value that choice, and choose something that is, perhaps, a lot more valuable.

NOTES:

_____

_____

_____

_____

_____

_____

WHAT'S YOUR HAPPINESS STRATEGY?

We put time into creating strategies for health, productivity, success, and relationships. Do we ever have a strategy for happiness? What can you do to cultivate happiness into life and into every other strategy you are working with? Truth is, that's your goal. You are trying to make more money because you think it will make you happier. Have you asked for happy? Focused on happy? Settled for nothing less than happy? If you have, great. You're ahead of the game. If not, then it may be time to strategize.

NOTES:

_____

_____

_____

_____

_____

_____

_____

_____

WHAT'S YOUR STORY?

Would you be willing to stop telling it? Would you be willing to change it? Would you be willing to never tell it again? We get very stuck in and attached to our stories. Then, we live them thinking they are real. How many of you have the story that you are poor or middle-classed? If you keep telling that story you will never be rich. How many of you have a story that you are a wounded victim? Keep telling that story, or keep trying to find the ending where justice is served, and you will always be living that story as the victim. How many of us have the story that we are right and know what's wrong with the world and everyone in it? Keep telling that one so that you will always be right that everything is wrong, and you will never have happiness. Is it time to let go of your stories?

NOTES:

_____

_____

_____

_____

_____

WHAT WOULD IT TAKE FOR YOU TO LIGHTEN YOUR MOOD?

We often get weighted down by the humdrum of the day, of work, and of life. Life was not meant to be humdrum. What would it take to lighten your mood? Would you be willing to let go of the martyr stance you may have taken to stay upset? Would you be willing to laugh at all the stuff you think you are supposed to be grumpy or upset about? Would you be willing to lighten up your mood for your own sake?

NOTES:

_____

_____

_____

_____

_____

_____

_____

_____

WHEN LIFE GIVES YOU ＿＿＿

When life gives you lemons, make lemonade. When life gives you shit, flush it away. How many people don't do that though? Instead, we lie there in it, telling people about it, saying, "Look at all the shit I've got. How come I've got shit and you don't have shit? It's not fair. You should have shit too." This is ridiculous when you look at it. When life gives you shit, clean it up. Flush it away. Find some lemons and make lemonade. Don't wallow, or complain, or keep talking about it. Change it. Clean it up and change it. Or else it just really stinks.

NOTES:

_____

_____

_____

_____

_____

_____

_____

WHERE ARE YOU HEADED?

No matter what is going on in your life know that you will be ok in the end. See yourself moving toward happiness, harmony, and contentment. If you can't, ask if you are preparing for a fight - a bloody, violent, awful, horrific fight or perhaps the opposite – a complete and utter failure. If so, would you like to change your mind? Would you like to surrender to some other possibility? Remember, always look to where you are going, not to where you have been. If you truly feel lightness, contentment, and harmony when you look forward, keep going. If you don't, you may want to change your mind and ask, "Is that really where I want to be headed?"

NOTES:

_____

_____

_____

_____

_____

_____

_____

WHO ARE YOU TRYING TO IMPRESS?

When you try to impress someone, it is like saying, "I'm not impressive," which is a complete and utter lie. Sometimes the most impressive thing is not needing to impress anyone. Would you be willing to let go of trying to be something, and instead, realize you are something? Don't try to impress. It will only lead you to disappointment. Instead, be unimpressive by being your plain, ordinary self, and you may just turn some heads.

NOTES:

_____

_____

_____

_____

_____

_____

_____

_____

_____

WHO DO YOU ANSWER TO?

Who do you answer to? If the answer is not to you, then you are giving your power and your choice away. You are the #1 authority in your life. If you answer to a higher power, it better include you. A higher power is not against you nor does it tell you what to do. A higher power will never judge you, which means there is nothing you "should" do. A higher power will always wish for you to do what you wish to do, and what would bring you the greatest expansion and joy. Answer to you today. Answer to the joy of you. There is no greater power than that.

NOTES:

_____

_____

_____

_____

_____

_____

_____

WHO'S GOT THE CON OF YOUR LIFE?

You know in Star Trek when the Captain would say, "I've got the con," and it meant they were in control of all decisions and choices? Who's got the con of your life? Is it you? If it's not, will you now proclaim, "I'VE GOT THE CON!" and relieve all others of their command? This is your life. Your life is your Starship Enterprise. Will you allow yourself to go where no one has ever gone before?

NOTES:

_____

_____

_____

_____

_____

_____

_____

_____

_____

_____

WHO'S GOT THE POWER? YOU DO.

You are more powerful than any judgment or criticism. You are more powerful than what you are letting control you. You just have to stand up and acknowledge that fact. It's not that you can't lighten up. You won't. It's not that you can't be happy either. You've just decided you can't. Nothing is making you upset. You're choosing it. That's how much power you have. Use it any way you wish.

NOTES:

WILL THIS MATTER IN 5 YEARS?

This is a great question to ask when you get wrapped up in the drama of everyday living. If this moment won't matter in 5 years, why make it matter now? Will it matter that your car broke down? Will it matter that you didn't get an A on the test? (Trust me, it won't matter). Will it matter that you had a fight with someone? Probably not. In 5 years time it will likely all be forgotten. So forget about it now. Choose happiness over upset. Choose gratitude over complaint. Why? Because if you do, it will make a difference to what your life becomes in 5 years.

NOTES:

_____

_____

_____

_____

_____

_____

_____

WINNING

Do you believe in order to win that everyone else has to lose? Do you realize everyone includes you? This means that in order for you to truly win, everyone else has to win too. What if we stopped competing to win, and started realizing winning must include everyone? What would change if you started focusing on everyone around you winning instead of losing? What if you included you in the mix too? Win-Win.

NOTES:

_____

_____

_____

_____

_____

_____

_____

_____

_____

WORTH

You are the pricer of you. We will often price ourselves as worthless, because we don't want people to turn us away. Ironically, by making ourselves worthless or less than, no one actually desires to have anything we have to contribute. Make yourself priceless, and everyone, including you, will see your value. As a bonus, being priceless means you never actually have to sell yourself or be owned by anyone else. You are just admired from near and afar.

NOTES:

_____

_____

_____

_____

_____

_____

_____

_____

WRITE

It is time to put pen to paper and write. Writing is an effective way to admit and face fears, which renders them powerless. It is also an effective way to gain insights directly from your soul. Write. Write whatever is coming to you. Write whatever it is you are afraid to say. Allow it to come out of you, be expressed through you, and provide you with healing. All the answers are within you. You just need to ask for them to come forth, and then write! You will be amazed what will be lifted off your chest, your shoulders and your mind! Lighten your load, and put it into paper. Do this today and notice how much better you feel.

NOTES:

_____

_____

_____

_____

_____

_____

_____

YOU ARE AWESOME!

How many times do you tell yourself this a day? Is it time to start telling the truth even if it hurts? You are AWESOME!!!! Sure, you want to prove that you aren't. You want to wallow in your problems or show how pathetic you can be, but there is no fooling me. There is only fooling yourself. Don't be a fool. Admit it. You are AWESOME!!!!

NOTES:

_____

_____

_____

_____

_____

_____

_____

_____

_____

_____

YOU ARE GIFTED

You are gifted and talented. If you don't think you are, you just aren't aware of what those gifts and talents are. Don't be fooled into thinking that you aren't masterful at something. Perhaps you are gifted at organization or at talking to people. Perhaps you are gifted at having compassion or forgiving others. Perhaps you are gifted in building things or understanding how things work. Do not underestimate your gifts or the importance they hold in this world. Do not sell your abilities short - especially those abilities that do not come with a university degree or a high profile job title. If you don't know your gifts, ask the Universe to show them to you. Don't forget to accept them when they are shown to you.

P.S. When you value your gifts, others will value them too – not before.

NOTES:

_____

_____

_____

_____

_____

YOU ARE LIVING BEAUTY

You are a living beauty filled with life that, when acknowledged, spills out from the inside and fills a room. Living energy is beautiful. It doesn't matter if it is in a flower, a tree, or you. When you feel alive, you exude an indefinable, exquisite quality. Be that today. Please don't deny the world of that beauty. To do so means you deny yourself of it as well.

NOTES:

_____

_____

_____

_____

_____

_____

_____

_____

_____

YOU ARE NOT A TEST TO PASS

Being you does not require you to jump through hurdles or be a certain way. You do not have to pass a test on how to be. You know how to be you. No one else does. How could anyone ever evaluate how well you are doing? How could anyone fail you when they can't even imagine how great you are? There is no test to pass. Stop trying to get it right. Stop looking to others as the evaluators of how you are doing. Be you and all will be well.

NOTES:

_____

_____

_____

_____

_____

_____

_____

_____

YOU ARE NOT TOO OLD

People will say, "I'd would have loved to learn to play the piano, but I'm too old now." or "I would love to know how to speak another language, but I'm too old now." Unless you have less than 3 weeks to live, you are not too old. You probably have 20-70 years of life left before you're dead. You can master anything in less than 20 years. What are you not doing because you think the time has passed? Is it time to acknowledge that you're a lot younger than you've been telling yourself? Is it time to realize you are never too old?

NOTES:

_____

_____

_____

_____

_____

_____

_____

_____

YOU ARE THE MIRACLE

What if you are the miracle you've been asking for? What is it that you haven't acknowledged about being a miracle? Would you be willing to even consider the possibility? Go about your day, exclaiming, "I am a miracle!" today. Amuse yourself with this notion. You may find more than you bargained for.

NOTES:

_____

_____

_____

_____

_____

_____

_____

_____

_____

YOU DO NOT WALK ALONE

You have consciousness with you always. Some claim it is a higher power, an inner power, or the Universe. It doesn't matter how you describe it. Just know you are never alone and always bathed in the love of consciousness. There is nothing to fear. Are you trying to do it on your own? Are you feeling like it is you against the world? Open to consciousness, and allow yourself to be surrounded by the wisdom, kindness, ease, and glory of the ages. It is there for you always.

NOTES:

_____

_____

_____

_____

_____

_____

_____

_____

YOU DON'T HAVE TO FIX TO CREATE

Many of us are trying to fix what's wrong in our lives instead of just creating something different. In order to have something different, you must create it different - not fix what you've got as if what you've got is broken. It's not broken. It's just what you don't want. So create. Make a change. Choose entirely differently. See what that does for you.

NOTES:

_____

_____

_____

_____

_____

_____

_____

_____

_____

YOU KNOW WHO YOU ARE

Who told you who you were? Or what you had to be? Were they correct? Did they make you feel wrong? Maybe it's because they were wrong. No one can tell you who or what you are. You are the only one who really knows. Don't let anyone else define you. And if you have, change your mind. Dismiss other's definitions of you. You are the only one who knows who you are. Stop being confused by others who don't know a damn thing about you.

NOTES:

_____

_____

_____

_____

_____

_____

_____

_____

_____

YOUR CHOICE TRUMPS EVERYTHING

You have a magical tool with you at all times - it's called your choice. When you choose something, truly choose, then nothing can stop its coming into existence. Nothing can override your choice. It's the trump card in the deck of possibilities. Choice requires unwavering trust in you. Know that if you choose something you wish you didn't, then you can choose again. There are no eternal ties to any one choice. What would you like to choose? Now, choose it. You have permission even though you don't need it. Go.

NOTES:

_____

_____

_____

_____

_____

_____

_____

_____

YOU'RE DIFFERENT

There is no one like you. You are one of a kind. Why are you trying to compare yourself with others? There's nothing to compare. You won't measure up to someone else, because the quality from person to person is so different that it is like comparing apples with celery. You're that different. Incomparable. Not remotely the same. Celebrate that and stop judging it.

NOTES:

_____

_____

_____

_____

_____

_____

_____

_____

_____

YOUR ISSUE IS NOT THE ISSUE

Whatever issue you have decided is your problem is not the problem. Thinking you have a problem is the problem. What if you focused on your situation not being a problem? Make it a non-issue. Then, you can no longer use it as the excuse that holds you back or keeps you a victim. Release your issues with issues. Focus on what you are creating, and not on why you can't create it. See what wondrous things may be created from that!

NOTES:

_____

_____

_____

_____

_____

_____

_____

ABOUT THE AUTHOR

Fay Thompson is a Strategist and Coach specializing in life and workplace happiness. She is also an international speaker and an Access Consciousness® Certified Facilitator. Fay spends her days writing, coaching individuals and businesses, and facilitating workshops. Her aim is to empower each person to realize their immense creative capacity and their ability to change anything into something greater or different.

Fay resides in Saskatchewan, Canada with her dazzling husband, two gorgeous children, loving dog, Elsa, and wise cat, Pluto.

To find out more about Fay and her work, or to book a coaching session or speaking engagement, visit www.faythompson.com.

You can also follow her on:

Facebook   www.facebook.com/faythompsoninspires

Instagram   www.instagram.com/faythompsoninspires

Manufactured by Amazon.ca
Bolton, ON